DECISIONS OF CONSEQUENCE

How U.S. Presidents Steered the World

Photos of presidents are from whitehouse.gov

Printed in the United States of America

ISBN 978-1-966136-12-5
eISBN 978-1-966136-23-1

Measure Publishing LLC
PO Box 9001 Mount Vernon, NY 10552

measurepub.com

32 31 30 29 28 27 26 01 02 03 04 05 06 07

AMERICAN HISTORY IN A NUTSHELL

DECISIONS OF CONSEQUENCE

How U.S. Presidents Steered the World

FORREST TOWER

Dedicated to MyRis, who is not a history buff by any means, but whose unwavering encouragement has made this book possible.

Also, thanks to my editor, Elisabeth Chretien, and friends Jessica Kreger and Amy Rose Spiegel for their excellent advice.

CONTENTS

PRESIDENTIAL FUN FACTS

ABOUT THE AMERICAN *HISTORY IN A NUTSHELL SERIES*

As we go through our educational experiences, most of us learn the basics of American history. Although these provide a foundation for our knowledge, there is more to every event you have read about. My goal is to provide insights into the critical junctures in the evolution of the American story in a way that interests you and makes you want to learn more.

I can remember the exact moment when I first became interested in American history. As a freshman in college, a friend handed me a book and said something to the effect that "I think you will really like this book." Which book was it? James Michner's Centennial. As a historical novel, it was so interesting, but even more important, it was educational. This book changed my life, and I was hooked on history. In college, I took as many elective American history courses as I could.

Although my educational background includes a B.S. in Biology and an M.S. in Management and Supervision, I have explored historical novels and non-fiction books on American history ever since reading James Michener's novel. I have read and studied many overviews and technical books on the country's founding, the Civil War, other seminal American events, as well as biographies of great Americans — especially Presidents — and other famous figures.

My career was in the pharmaceutical and medical device fields. Starting in pharmaceutical sales, I advanced into a range of management roles at three of the largest drug companies. After the last company I worked for was acquired, I voluntarily left and started a health care consulting business focused on health economics. I spent almost 40 years in the pharmaceutical/medical world and then retired. I soon realized that many of the skills I developed during my working years were transferable to research and writing. After reading a few quick-read American history books, I thought to myself, "I can do this," and thus began my writing adventure.

My first foray into writing is a series of books with the overarching scope: "American History In A Nutshell." Using this moniker, there are many avenues of American history to explore. The objective is not just to present American history in the usual textbook fashion. Instead, I want to offer my readers easy-to-read, entertaining, microlearning books. Each book is designed so the reader can pick it up and read a snippet (chapter) in just a few moments, either sequentially or individually, and get something out of it. A fact, a story, or an idea that you can tell your friend, partner, or convey at a party. These books are meant to make history approachable, memorable, and fun, while also offering thought-provoking concepts that take readers back in time.

Whether it's about how American leaders make decisions, their greatest successes and failures, what they said, or the known and unknown men and women who founded the nation, these books offer readers new, thought-provoking ways to enjoy American history. For example, a future book, The U.S. Supreme Court: Decisions of Consequence, takes the reader through the history of the most critical and meaningful Supreme Court cases, as "told" by the Chief Justices. In each of my books, I also take you on a journey on how each subject impacted American society. This way, you can relate to how these historical events affected the country then and now.

I hope you learn something from my writings, and, more importantly, that you learn to love American history as much as I do. Enjoy!

Forrest Tower, January, 2026

INTRODUCTION

"The land of the free and the home of the brave" did not just happen by itself. It was conceived, created, crafted, and molded into the country we know today. Using the framework the Founding Fathers gave us through the Constitution, each president has been given unique powers and responsibilities and, accordingly, had to make important decisions in order to handle a crisis or achieve a political agenda.

Certainly, every president makes decisions, as the role requires a president to manage issues that are national or international in scope. As the chief executive of the executive branch, the president signs legislation into law, vetoes bills, negotiates treaties, and issues executive orders. The President appoints federal judges and, most importantly, nominates justices to the Supreme Court. Through the Department of Justice, the president is responsible for implementing and enforcing federal laws. The president is also the commander-in-chief of the US Armed Forces.

But which decisions are the most important? Are they foreign or domestic? Which affects the greatest number of Americans or people around the world, either positively or negatively? These are decisions of consequence, the subject of this book.

Presidential dealings with economic ups and downs, peace and war, civil rights and other social and political matters helped shape American history. Decision after decision built upon one another, forming our culture, and will hopefully continue to lead us to a "more perfect union."

Presidents do not make consequential decisions in a vacuum. They depend on the advice of political consultants, cabinet members, and subject-matter experts; they listen to public opinion; and they are limited by the Constitutional system of checks and balances.

This book came about through the reading of its author, a history buff. In his reading, he came across two especially interesting books that inspired this manuscript. The first, a small compendium of American history, describes important events in US history on a single page. American History in Bite-Sized Chunks by Alison Rattle and Allison Vale employs a concise, bite-sized format, which this book emulates. The second book of significance is The Situation Room: The Inside Story of Presidents in Crisis by George Stephanopoulos. In his book, Stephanopoulos describes numerous instances when presidents from Kennedy to the present day have needed the unique resources—including access to national or international events or information—of the Situation Room to make informed decisions, sometimes of monumental consequence.

Thus, the concept of a book that relates each president's decision of consequence in an easy-to-read format was born.

Of course, the selection of Decisions of Consequence is somewhat subjective. Using various search engines, including AI, the author searched for the most consequential decisions made by each president and why they were so significant. Decisions were selected where there was overlap in the responses from the searches, and then further research was conducted to understand the context and implications better.

GEORGE WASHINGTON

FIRST PRESIDENT
ONLY US PRESIDENT UNAFFILIATED WITH A POLITICAL PARTY
TERM: 1789–1797
YEAR OF THE DECISION: 1797

CIRCUMSTANCE

George Washington was the military commander of the US forces during the American Revolutionary War and the country's first president. The country was just forming when he assumed office, with the states ratifying the Constitution in 1788, just before he was elected. Washington was unanimously elected as our first president. Accordingly, he had to decide how to structure his new government and define the role of the executive branch. He formed the first Cabinet by selecting a group of diverse and often contrarian thinkers, including Alexander Hamilton and Thomas Jefferson. Washington founded the Supreme Court of the United States and established the judicial system's multitiered structure to administer equal justice to all. Our country's economic structure, with a strong centralized government system, was devised, and the US Mint was established under Washington's rule. During Washington's term, the Bill of Rights was added to the Constitution. On the foreign policy side, Washington set forth a position of US neutrality regarding global events.

When Washington was president, there was no limit on how many terms a US president could serve. This led to what is perhaps Washington's most important decision.

DECISION

After serving two four-year terms, Washington decided to forgo becoming a president-for-life and instead left office. Thus, he peacefully transferred the power of the presidency back to the American people and their elected officials, including a new president.

IMPACT

By voluntarily stepping down, Washington demonstrated that the presidency was not a lifetime position, as in a monarchy, and that the new government could function without a continuous leader. He unofficially established term limits by retiring after his second term, a tradition that continued until Franklin D. Roosevelt was elected for third and fourth terms in the 1930s and 1940s. Eventually, in 1951, the two-term precedent established by Washington was codified into the US Constitution.

By leaving office after two terms, Washington established the crucial function of the peaceful transfer of power to a duly elected individual to serve as the president. This principle has endured since his tenure, although there have been a few instances of some concern.

JOHN ADAMS

SECOND PRESIDENT
FEDERALIST PARTY
TERM: 1797–1801
YEAR OF THE DECISION: 1797

CIRCUMSTANCE

John Adams, the second US president, succeeded George Washington and took office in 1797. He served only a single term. In the closely contested election of 1796, he won the presidency with seventy-one electoral votes; his competitor, Thomas Jefferson, received sixty-eight. Under the original electoral system, the candidate with the second-highest number of electoral votes became the vice president. Thus, Jefferson served as Adams's vice president.

During his tenure, Adams signed the Alien and Sedition Acts of 1798, which were controversial laws that made it harder for immigrants to become citizens and allowed the government to imprison or deport non-citizens it deemed dangerous. The Sedition Act also criminalized making false statements critical of the federal government. Adams believed in having a strong navy and, while maintaining a general position of neutrality, built up this branch of the military. In 1800, Adams was the first to reside in the White House, although it was simply known as the President's House at the time. Late in his term, Adams nominated and pushed through the appointments of many judges known to support the ideologies of his party, the Federalists.

Following the revolution in France in 1789, relations between the US and the new French government were initially friendly but soon became strained. France and Great Britain went to war in 1792, but President Washington declared American neutrality in the conflict. Although the US was neutral, both France and Britain seized US ships that traded with their enemies. The US entered a trade agreement with Britain in 1795, which angered France. Accordingly, the French Navy ramped up its efforts to prevent American trade with Britain. By the time Adams took office, the matter was reaching crisis proportions.

Popular opinion on the matter was broadly divided along political lines. Adams's party, the Federalists, favored a defensive buildup but not necessarily outright war. Jefferson's Democratic-Republicans sympathized with the ideals of the French revolutionaries and did not want to be seen as cooperating with the Federalists on this matter.

The US sent three of its Founding Fathers to France to negotiate a solution. However, they refused to submit the customary bribes for an audience with France's Foreign Minister, Talleyrand. They were subsequently sent back to the United States, infuriating officials in the Adams administration.

Adams called the first special session of Congress to address the deteriorating state of French–American relations. Adams released the diplomatic correspondence to Congress, replacing the names of the French intermediaries with X, Y, and Z. Hence, the name the XYZ Affair. This action stirred up American public opinion against France, generating substantial anti-French sentiment.

Ultimately, Adams sent another peace mission to France. This led to the signing of the Convention of 1800, also known as the Treaty of Mortefontaine, which restored peace between the two nations.

DECISION

Although the Federalists called for war, Adams decided to follow Washington's position of neutrality and chose not to seek a declaration of war against France. Simultaneously, he endeavored to build up the US military and substantially strengthened the US Navy.

In 1799, President Adams sent negotiators to France, and they eventually negotiated an end to hostilities in September 1800. Interestingly, the agreement was made with France's First Consul, Napoleon Bonaparte.

IMPACT

While the decision to remain officially neutral kept the XYZ Affair from escalating into a full-blown war with France, skirmishes between the two countries' navies ensued, mostly in the Caribbean. This undeclared naval conflict was known as the Quasi-War and lasted from 1798 to 1800. By creating the US Department of the Navy, commissioning additional frigates, and enlisting at least ten thousand additional soldiers, Adams positioned the United States as a military power. This led the French to realize that an outright war would be costly, and eventually, France engaged in treaty negotiations.

The XYZ Affair deepened the partisan divide between Federalists and Democratic-Republicans, who remained skeptical of the affair and continued to support France. Adams's actions related to the XYZ Affair played a significant role in his reelection loss to Thomas Jefferson.

THOMAS JEFFERSON

THIRD PRESIDENT
DEMOCRATIC-REPUBLICAN PARTY
TERM: 1801–1809
YEAR OF THE DECISION: 1803

CIRCUMSTANCE

Thomas Jefferson is forever known as the eloquent writer of the Declaration of Independence. He held definitive views on how the new nation should be structured, including limiting the power of the federal government, supporting states' rights to govern themselves, emphasizing individual liberties and the separation of church and state, and a strict interpretation of the Constitution without broad extrapolations that could strengthen the federal government. And yet, his most consequential decision as president was unrelated to these issues.

Following the XYZ Affair with France during John Adams's tenure, the country was greatly concerned about French influence and power. Then, in 1800, Spain secretly ceded the Louisiana Territory back to France. This move greatly alarmed the Americans, who were particularly concerned about having uninterrupted access to the Port of New Orleans and the Mississippi River, which was critical to American commerce.

At the time, Napoleon, the ruler of France, was trying to increase French influence and power in the Western Hemisphere; however, a new war between Britain and France was brewing. France's finance minister advised Napoleon that Louisiana was in a precarious position and could be captured by Britain via Canada.

Jefferson sent Robert Livingston to Paris to negotiate for the purchase of New Orleans and possibly parts of Florida. Future President James Monroe was later sent to aid the negotiations.

Unexpectedly, France's Foreign Minister, Talleyrand, offered to sell the entire Louisiana Territory to the United States. The offer exceeded the original scope of the American negotiation position.

DECISION

Jefferson's critical decision was to acquire the enormous swath of land from France in what was known as the Louisiana Purchase. The treaty was signed for $15 million—about $420 million in today's dollars—and it practically doubled the size of the United States. The purchase added 827,000 square miles to the US.

IMPACT

The Louisiana Purchase was notable for several reasons.

First, it dramatically increased the United States's geographical reach, extending its borders from the Mississippi River to the Rocky Mountains. The newly acquired land held huge quantities of natural resources and fertile agricultural areas, giving the young nation enormous economic potential.

This purchase also guaranteed that the US would control both the Mississippi River and the Port of New Orleans. This was critically important for the economy, as it protected both American trade and national security. The US could now fortify an important seaport entrance to the midwestern section of the US and beyond.

Without the Louisiana Purchase, the Lewis and Clark Expedition would not have happened or even been necessary. They explored the new territory and paved the way for westward expansion.

Jefferson was concerned that his strict interpretation of the Constitution conflicted with the purchase. He overcame his concerns by rationalizing that the land purchase would bring tremendous benefits to the country and that the Constitution charged him with acting in the country's best interests.

As the defining decision of the Jefferson presidency, the Louisiana Purchase helped shape the future of the United States by creating an opportunity for expansion. It offered great economic potential and helped turn the US into a true continental power. Thus, it had far-reaching importance for American politics, economics, and geography, which continues to influence the nation to this day.

JAMES MADISON

FOURTH PRESIDENT
DEMOCRATIC-REPUBLICAN PARTY
TERM: 1809–1817
YEAR OF THE DECISION: 1812

CIRCUMSTANCE

The United States' fourth president is known as the father of the Constitution. He also wrote the first ten amendments, known as the Bill of Rights. A close ally of Thomas Jefferson, both of whom were from Virginia, Madison served as Jefferson's Secretary of State.

During Madison's time as president, the British interfered with US commerce and impressed American sailors into the Royal Navy. They also supported Native American efforts to thwart westward expansion, particularly under the leadership of Tecumseh, a famous tribal leader.

The idea of going to war with Great Britain was highly controversial, particularly in New England, where trade with Britain was a significant economic factor. Nonetheless, Madison was determined to end Britain's interference in the fledgling country's economy.

DECISION

Madison asked Congress to declare war on Britain on June 1, 1812, which started the War of 1812.

IMPACT

The decision to go to war with Britain had major consequences. It tested the American resolve to defend itself; however, the initial phases of the war did not go well. In fact, the British invaded and burnt two of the three seats of the US government: the Capitol and the White House.

Eventually, the tide turned, and US forces achieved several major victories. Of particular importance was Andrew Jackson's triumph at the Battle of New Orleans in 1815. It helped turn public opinion and boost national pride. This battle made Jackson a national hero and future president.

Although the War of 1812 resulted in a draw, with no clear winner, the world had now seen that America could hold its ground and defend itself from interference by a great power. This in itself was a victory for President Madison, which made him and his party extremely popular, built political unity, and destroyed their primary opposition, the Federalist Party.

There were no changes in territory from the War of 1812 with Britain. However, there were improvements in America's national confidence, and the public became more unified. Native American power declined in the northwest, and Canada's national identity was strengthened.

JAMES MONROE

FIFTH PRESIDENT
DEMOCRATIC-REPUBLICAN PARTY
TERM: 1817–1825
YEAR OF THE DECISION: 1823

CIRCUMSTANCE

Monroe was a native Virginian and the last of the Founding Fathers to be elected president. He studied at the College of William and Mary but left to serve in the Revolutionary War. He was severely wounded in the Battle of Trenton. His presidency is associated with the Era of Good Feelings, a period marked by national unity and the decline of partisan politics. International affairs, however, eventually changed the peaceful climate.

Spain's colonization of Latin America was collapsing. During the Napoleonic Wars, many Spanish colonies in South America gained their independence. There were fears that other great European powers would swoop in to fill the void and recolonize these newly formed countries. Also, Russia was making territorial claims on the northwestern coast of the Americas at this time.

President Monroe was greatly concerned about

European influence and military presence in the Western Hemisphere.

DECISION

In his inaugural address, James Monroe declared that the Western Hemisphere was essentially closed to European colonization and strongly cautioned against interference with the new Latin American countries. This policy became enshrined as the Monroe Doctrine.

IMPACT

The Monroe Doctrine effectively stated to the world that the Western Hemisphere was the United States's sphere of influence. It positioned the US as the dominant country in the Americas. This doctrine became a cornerstone of US foreign policy, helping to shape policy towards international relations to the present day.

Monroe asserted America's separation from European affairs and demonstrated the nation's growing strength.

This doctrine has endured over time and been applied in many ways by subsequent presidents, demonstrating its adaptability to changing geopolitical environments.

JOHN QUINCY ADAMS

SIXTH PRESIDENT
DEMOCRATIC-REPUBLICAN PARTY
TERM: 1825–1829
YEAR OF THE DECISION: 1825

CIRCUMSTANCE

The candidates for the 1824 presidency included Andrew Jackson and John Quincy Adams, the son of former President John Adams. However, William Crawford and Henry Clay were also strong contenders. Andrew Jackson secured the most popular votes and also the most Electoral College votes (ninety-nine), while Adams came in second with eighty-four. Neither candidate held the majority of the total electoral votes, which was required to win the presidency. In such a situation, the Twelfth Amendment stipulated that the House of Representatives would determine the outcome of the election. Under these rules, each state had one vote, which could be cast for one of the top three candidates: Jackson, Adams, or Crawford.

On February 9, 1825, Adams received thirteen state votes; Jackson, seven; and Crawford, four. Thus, Adams was elected the sixth president of the United States.

After being eliminated from the House election, Henry Clay endorsed Adams, giving John Quincy Adams the House votes needed to win. Following his election, Adams appointed Clay the Secretary of State.

The controversial results of the House election angered Andrew Jackson's supporters, who claimed that Clay had thrown his support behind Adams in exchange for the Cabinet position. The term "Corrupt Bargain" was thus coined and affected Adams throughout his presidency.

DECISION

The most important decision John Quincy Adams made as president was appointing Henry Clay as his Secretary of State. This decision had far-reaching consequences that shaped Adams's presidency and political legacy.

IMPACT

From the start of his presidency, the accusation of there being a "Corrupt Bargain" undermined Adams's authority, as many, especially supporters of Jackson, believed that he was elected illegitimately. This cloud of suspicion weakened Adams politically. Jackson and his followers formed a new political party, the Democrats, and they immediately began to block the legislative initiatives of Adams's agenda, which limited the number and scope of his administration's accomplishments.

After the formation of the Democratic Party, the National Republican Party, which later became the Whig Party, was formed. This created the two-party system. Adams lost the following election to Andrew Jackson, primarily due to the "Corrupt Bargain," which resulted in him serving only a single term as president.

ANDREW JACKSON

SEVENTH PRESIDENT
DEMOCRATIC PARTY
TERM: 1829–1837
YEAR OF THE DECISION: 1840

CIRCUMSTANCE

More than any president before him, Andrew Jackson's goal was to represent the common man.

Prior to becoming president, Jackson was a major general, having defeated the British in the Battle of New Orleans during the War of 1812. Due to his exceptional toughness, endurance, resilience, and unyielding character, Jackson earned the nickname "Old Hickory."

Although he won the popular vote and had more electoral college votes than any other candidate in the 1824 election, he did not have the majority of them, which was required to win the presidency. The election was thus cast into the House of Representatives, which elected John Quincy Adams. In 1828, however, Jackson defeated Adams in a landslide victory.

Andrew Jackson survived the first assassination attempt against a US president.

Jackson is known for many notable acts, including the Indian Relocation Act, recognizing the Republic of Texas, issuing the Nullification Proclamation, which asserted federal superiority over state laws, and being the only president to pay off the national debt. While this was important, another issue related to national finance was even more critical.

In 1816, following the War of 1812, the economy of the United States was unstable. The war left the country in debt, and foreign trade had been disrupted. Congress attempted to strengthen the economy by creating a national bank, which would create a single paper currency for the country. At the time, each state had chartered banks with their own currency.

The bank was commissioned with handling all financial transactions for the US government, including holding and transferring deposits, processing tax payments, and managing government transactions. The bank had twenty-five branches throughout the country, including in the outskirts, which was meant to enable and enhance economic growth by providing credit to businesses and farmers. Another goal of the bank was to stabilize public credit issued through private banks.

The Second Bank of the United States succeeded the First Bank of the United States, which was created by Alexander Hamilton but had closed in 1811.

Concerns about corruption and mismanagement arose after the bank made large, often nonperforming loans to insiders and friends. The bank's lack of oversight enabled risky and corrupt practices, nearly leading it into bankruptcy just two years into its existence.

President Jackson was a strong opponent of the bank,

as he believed it favored the wealthy and did not serve the interests of the ordinary people.

DECISION

In 1832, Jackson expanded the scope of presidential authority by vetoing the renewal of the charter of the Second Bank of the United States. He cited the bank's unconstitutionality and potential danger to public liberty and states' rights. He removed all federal government deposits from the Second Bank and had them placed in state banks. This significantly reduced the bank's size and ability to influence the nation's currency and credit.

IMPACT

Congress tried and failed to override Jackson's veto. The controversy significantly weakened the pro-bank Whig Party, which had been created to oppose Jackson, and they lost Congressional seats in the 1843 elections.

Failing to be rechartered, the Second Bank became a private corporation bank in Pennsylvania, thus ending its responsibilities as a federal bank.

The absence of a federal bank created a void in the national banking system, leading to economic instability and volatility. The closure created "pet banks," which were the numerous private banks chartered within each state that thus lacked uniform regulations. This led to a boom-and-bust period, with a severe economic depression in 1837.

Prior to Jackson's veto of the Second Bank, presidents had used the veto power very sparingly, typically only for Constitutional issues. Jackson's use of the veto for economic reasons created a new dynamic between presidents and Congress.

It would be more than eighty years before the Federal Reserve System, a new national banking system, would come to fruition in 1913.

MARTIN VAN BUREN

EIGHTH PRESIDENT
DEMOCRATIC PARTY
TERM: 1837–1841
YEAR OF THE DECISION: 1840

CIRCUMSTANCE

In 1837, the United States was in the throes of the worst economic depression in its history to date. It began just three months into Van Buren's presidency and was called the Panic of 1837. During this time, many businesses and half of all banks failed due to bank runs on deposits, causing great hardship on the population. Unemployment was high, and many lost their lands.

A collapsing land bubble, a dramatic decline in cotton prices, speculative lending in the West, the movement of precious metals between countries as a result of international trade imbalances, and restrictive lending policies in Britain combined to trigger the depression.

Van Buren was a devotee of Jefferson and Jackson. He embraced a political philosophy of limited federal government, while also protecting individual liberties. His reluctance to initiate strong federal economic interventions is believed to have extended the depression much longer than was necessary.

Rather than acknowledging the role Jackson's economic policies had played in the depression—policies Van Buren had supported—he blamed the crisis on greedy American and foreign business and financial institutions, for which he was criticized.

Van Buren was widely condemned for not implementing emergency relief measures or stimulating the economy through infrastructure projects, which would have increased employment.

DECISION

Van Buren proposed establishing an independent treasury system to handle government transactions. This system would be separate from the existing one, which allowed for the mixing of governmental and private funds. Protecting government funds from the poorly managed state banking structure would reduce the likelihood of government monies being lost in bank failures, thus reducing the influence of banks on the economy.

IMPACT

Congress was reluctant to pass the legislation to create an independent treasury. After all, Andrew Jackson had vetoed the renewal of the charter of the Second Bank, which probably would have addressed the Panic quickly and helped resolve the dire economic situation. In 1840, three years after the Panic of 1837, Van Buren's concept was finally approved.

The independent treasury system laid the groundwork for how the government would handle its finances in the future, separating government funds from private banks.

Van Buren's handling of the economic crisis, including the independent treasury proposal, was widely criticized and led to his losing the 1840 election. He left office as a discredited president.

The Whigs won the 1840 election and promptly repealed the Treasury Law, which had been passed only a year earlier. Despite it being repealed, the notion of an independent treasury system had a lasting impact and was reestablished in 1846. This functioned until the Federal Reserve System replaced it in 1913.

WILLIAM HENRY HARRISON

NINTH PRESIDENT
WHIG PARTY
TERM: 1841
YEAR OF THE DECISION: 1841

CIRCUMSTANCE

William Henry Harrison, a great war hero from the Battle of Tippecanoe, served only one month in office before succumbing to pneumonia. He was the first president to die in office. Although he had been sick with a cold prior to his inauguration, Harrison gave a lengthy inaugural address in cold, wet weather, which likely contributed to his death. As such, he did not have many opportunities to make decisions of consequence.

Perhaps his most important consequential action was delivering the longest inaugural address, lasting almost two hours. During this speech, he outlined his vision for the country, which included sticking with Whig Party principles by limiting executive power and deferring to Congress on many matters. In this regard, he criticized what he considered to be overreach by past presidents, especially related to fiscal policy. Additionally, he promised to use his veto power only for laws that he believed would be unconstitutional. With respect to slavery, he was in favor of states' rights.

DECISION

Notably, Harrison promised to be a transitional president and serve only for a single term.

IMPACT

The decision to serve a single term supported the Whig Party's position of limited executive power. It solidified his loyalty to the Whig platform, which supported term limits and limiting presidential power. Had he survived his term, William Henry Harrison would have made decisions based on his principles, without concerns about reelection.

JOHN TYLER

TENTH PRESIDENT
WHIG PARTY
TERM: 1841–1845
YEAR OF THE DECISION: 1841

CIRCUMSTANCE

Following the unexpected death of President William Henry Harrison, the responsibilities of the vice president were uncertain, as Harrison was the first to die in office. It was a hotly debated question: Should the vice president become an acting president with limited authority until a duly elected president was confirmed, or should the vice president assume the full responsibilities of the president? The Constitution did not clearly define this role. As such, Tyler became the "Accidental President" and had to decide for himself and future vice presidents what level of authority he should assume.

DECISION

Insisting that he was not a caretaker, Tyler asserted that he was entitled to the full powers and responsibilities of the presidency. He took the Oath of Office and moved into the White House. These actions established that upon the death of a president, the vice president ascends to the full presidency for the remainder of the term.

IMPACT

In deciding to assume full presidential authority following Harrison's death, Tyler fundamentally shaped the American presidency, the orderly transfer of power, the continuity of government, and the overall stability of the US government. These actions reassured US political bodies, the public at large, and international powers that the US had a functioning, fully empowered chief executive and commander-in-chief.

Although Tyler assumed the full authority of the presidency, he made a costly mistake by vetoing the revival of the National Bank. This decision led to his expulsion from the Whig Party and his inability to garner the necessary political support to win another term in office.

JAMES POLK

ELEVENTH PRESIDENT
DEMOCRATIC PARTY
TERM: 1845–1849
YEAR OF THE DECISION: 1848

CIRCUMSTANCE

James Polk entered office with a clear expansionist agenda grounded in the concept of Manifest Destiny, the belief that it was the United States's "destiny" to expand across the North American continent. Polk aimed to annex Texas and acquire New Mexico and California from Mexico. Diplomatic efforts failed to achieve this purchase, and Polk took steps that led to war with Mexico. He sent General Zachary Taylor to the disputed area on the Rio Grande, which antagonized Mexican troops and led to an attack on Taylor's forces. Polk then asked Congress to declare war on Mexico.

The US won a decisive victory against Mexico, which resulted in Mexico's acquiescence to the US purchase of New Mexico and California for $15 million ($600 million today). The acquisition dramatically increased the size of the United States, and now the country spanned from the Atlantic to the Pacific Ocean, which provided the nation a strategic advantage. This expansion also caused an increase in the bitter tensions between the North and South. Would they be slave or free states? The aftermath of the war with Mexico caused a shift in political alliances, weakening the existing party system and paving the way for the rise of the Republican Party.

DECISION

Polk's annexation of Texas amplified animosities between Mexico and the United States, which resulted in the Mexican-American War.

IMPACT

The annexation of Texas and the US victory in the Mexican-American War led to the acquisition of large territories in the Southwest and along the Pacific Coast, which in turn led to the creation of the Department of the Interior.

Relations with Mexico remained strained; however, the Mexican-American War gave valuable combat experience to many who would go on to fight in the Civil War.

With the acquisition of California, the US gained access to vast mineral wealth, especially gold, and to the Pacific Ocean. California became a state in 1850, further dividing the country and complicating the balance between slave-owning and free states.

ZACHARY TAYLOR

TWELFTH PRESIDENT
WHIG PARTY
TERM: 1849–1850
YEAR OF THE DECISION: 1849

CIRCUMSTANCE

Zachary Taylor was a general and national hero in the United States Army, distinguished by his service in the Mexican-American War and the War of 1812. He spent forty years in the Army, which caused him to hold strong nationalist positions. His nickname, "Old Rough and Ready," derived from his homespun ways that were politically appealing. His long military record was attractive to Northerners, while his ownership of a hundred slaves lured Southern voters. Before the election, Taylor had not committed himself one way or another on the troublesome issue of slavery.

In a three-way election between the Whigs, the Democrats, and the newly formed Free-Soil Party, which nominated Martin Van Buren, Taylor was the victor and was elected president.

Following the Mexican-American War, Taylor was

open to the rapid admission of New Mexico and California as new states. While Southern states wanted the new territories to be slave-owning, Northern states were strongly opposed to this. Despite the possibility of Southern secession from the Union over this issue, Taylor was committed to holding the nation together, even if it meant using force.

In February 1850, Southern leaders met with Taylor in a heated conference in which they threatened secession. He told them that, if it was necessary to enforce the law, he would personally lead the Army against them. He warned that persons "taken in rebellion against the Union, he would hang…with less reluctance than he had hanged deserters and spies in Mexico." He never wavered.

In July 1850, Taylor took ill following a ceremony at the Washington Monument on a frigid day. He passed away five days later.

DECISION

Taylor encouraged settlers in California and New Mexico to draft constitutions and apply for statehood, thus bypassing the territorial stage for admission into the Union. Their constitutions ought to address slavery directly. Through the Compromise of 1850, which was passed following Taylor's death, much of his political agenda was achieved.

IMPACT

Taylor thought his decision would likely result in New Mexico and California being admitted as free states, thereby upsetting the delicate balance between free and slave states in the Senate. Although Taylor was opposed to the Compromise of 1850, California did achieve statehood in that year. New Mexico, on the other hand, repeatedly attempted to become a state but did not do so until 1912.

The Compromise of 1850 included the admission of California to the Union as a free state. It also strengthened the Fugitive Slave Act, which required the federal government to assist in capturing and returning runaway slaves. It banned the trading of slaves in Washington, DC, but allowed slave owners to continue to have slaves. It established New Mexico and Utah as territories with no requirement that they be free, leaving the decision of slavery to the settlers of the territories. The compromise also had the federal government assume some of the debt that the former State of Texas owed in exchange for its rescinding its claims to certain lands, thereby redefining its borders.

Many Southerners perceived Taylor, a slaveholder himself, as an ally in expanding slavery to the new territories and were extremely disappointed with his position of adding new free states to the country.

The decision demonstrated Taylor's commitment to preserving the Union over the proprietary interests of the slave states, despite his own background as a Southern slaveholder. The concept of Union preservation at all costs would impact the country significantly in the coming decades.

MILLARD FILLMORE

THIRTEENTH PRESIDENT
WHIG PARTY
TERM: 1850–1853
YEAR OF THE DECISION: 1850

CIRCUMSTANCE

Upon the untimely death of Zachary Taylor, Millard Fillmore ascended to the presidency while Congress was arguing ferociously over the admission of new states as free or slave-owning. As vice president, Fillmore had presided over the Senate during the months of strenuous debate that ultimately led to the Compromise of 1850. Although he made no public comment on the merits of the Compromise's proposals, he intimated to President Taylor that if there should be a tie vote on the bill, he would vote in favor of it. Then, suddenly, Taylor died, and it was up to Fillmore to decide whether to support or oppose the proposed legislation. He endorsed it and signed it into law.

Interestingly, Fillmore was the last president to be elected from a party other than the Democratic or Republican parties.

DECISION

The Compromise of 1850 was actually a series of bills designed to ease tensions between the Northern and Southern states over the issue of slavery, particularly in newly acquired territories. As the new president, Fillmore decided that it was in the country's best interest to enact the Compromise of 1850, which had favorable elements for both the pro-slavery Southern states and the abolitionist Northern states.

IMPACT

Fillmore supported and signed the Compromise of 1850 to preserve the Union and prevent a civil war. Fillmore's support was critical in getting the legislation passed through Congress.

Enacting the Compromise of 1850 temporarily prevented the secession of Southern states and preserved the Union.

FRANKLIN PIERCE

FOURTEENTH PRESIDENT
DEMOCRATIC PARTY
TERM: 1853–1857
YEAR OF THE DECISION: 1854

CIRCUMSTANCE

Franklin Pierce was a former senator from New Hampshire. His running mate was from Alabama. Pierce was a dark-horse candidate who won the Democratic nomination on the forty-ninth ballot at the Democratic National Convention.

The 1852 election was a three-way race and ended up being a landslide victory for the forty-seven-year-old Franklin Pierce. He secured 254 electoral votes to his closest competitor's forty-two. After the Compromise of 1850, Pierce hoped to preside over an era of peace, as both the Whigs and the Democrats were satisfied with the legislation. Pierce, a New Englander, had an open mind regarding the recommendations of his Southern advisers. He wanted to prevent another bitter disagreement over slavery. However, rather than maintaining peace, his policies actually exacerbated the country's disruption.

Southern advisors suggested that he sign the Kansas-Nebraska Act, which greatly appeased and favored Southern slave states. This Act would create the Territories of Kansas and Nebraska and let them decide the question of slavery for themselves through a popular vote.

DECISION

The most crucial decision Franklin Pierce made as president was signing the Kansas-Nebraska Act into law on May 30, 1854.

IMPACT

This Act had several major consequences. It effectively repealed the Missouri Compromise of 1820, which had prohibited slavery in territories in the north. Pierce eventually agreed to support the explicit repeal of the Missouri Compromise instead of allowing the issue to go to the Supreme Court.

It permitted "popular sovereignty," allowing white male settlers in the Kansas and Nebraska Territories to determine whether to allow slavery. This caused intense conflict, especially in Kansas, where it sparked a period known as "Bleeding Kansas," where pro-slavery and anti-slavery settlers engaged in violent confrontations.

More generally, the legislation deepened the divides between the North and South. It intensified Northern anti-slavery sentiment and is considered a significant catalyst for events leading to the Civil War.

Finally, the Kansas-Nebraska Act severely damaged Pierce's political standing, which contributed to his party's refusal to renominate him for a second term. It also contributed to the eventual collapse of the Whig Party and the rise of the Republican Party.

JAMES BUCHANAN

FIFTEENTH PRESIDENT
DEMOCRATIC PARTY
TERM: 1857–1861
YEAR OF THE DECISION: 1860

CIRCUMSTANCE

James Buchanan was the first bachelor president, and his niece, Harriet Lane, served as the First Lady. Buchanan served at a time when the Union was sharply divided over slavery. The political parties were in a state of disarray, as the Democrats were divided, the Whigs were largely destroyed, and the Republican Party was emerging. Before becoming president, Buchanan had a long political career, including serving in the House of Representatives and the Senate, as Polk's Secretary of State, and as Minister to Russia and the United Kingdom. As a foreign diplomat, Buchanan was largely insulated from American political hostilities.

Buchanan incorrectly thought the political divide would resolve itself if he appointed a balanced Cabinet. He also thought he could persuade political leaders and the population to accept Constitutional law as the Supreme Court interpreted it.

At the time of his election, the nation's highest court was taking on the issue of slavery and was considering the legality of restricting slavery in the new territories. Two justices hinted to Buchanan what the decision would be, leading him to comment on the subject in his inaugural address.

In that address, Buchanan referred to slavery as "a matter of but little practical importance," as he believed that the Supreme Court would imminently be deciding the issue and that it would be resolved.

Two days later, in the Dred Scott decision, the Supreme Court determined that Congress did not have the Constitutional authority to deprive persons of their property rights—in other words, slaves—in the new territories. Southerners were delighted that the Court had ruled in their favor, but the North was furious.

Buchanan supported the admission of Kansas as a slave state; however, this position angered the Republicans and further divided his own Democratic Party. In the end, Kansas remained a territory and did not achieve full statehood under Buchanan's tenure.

In the midterm elections of 1858, the Republicans won a plurality, but the Southern bloc and presidential vetoes against Southern-proposed legislation supporting slavery effectively stalled the government. In the next presidential election, the Democrats were so severely divided that they ran two separate candidates, one from the North and one from the South, splitting the party.

DECISION

Toward the end of his presidency, Buchanan took steps to legally prevent the Southern states from seceding while simultaneously claiming that the federal government did not possess the legal authority to prevent secession.

IMPACT

Buchanan's indecisiveness exacerbated tensions between the North and South, seemingly encouraging the Southern states to secede from the Union. When he decided that the federal government could not prevent secession, he positioned the government as militarily weak. He refused to fortify federal government forts, still hopeful that a peaceful settlement could be reached. This set the stage for the American Civil War.

Buchanan's inability to prevent Southern secession and his poor leadership during the entire crisis have led many historians to rank him as one of the worst US presidents.

ABRAHAM LINCOLN

SIXTEENTH PRESIDENT
REPUBLICAN PARTY
TERM: 1861–1865
YEAR OF THE DECISION: 1863

CIRCUMSTANCE

In 1863, the Civil War was in its third bloody year. Being a savvy politician, Lincoln seized a strategic opportunity to free the slaves, make their freedom an explicit military goal of the Civil War, and also prevent the secession of any additional slave states.

At the time, the Union Army was struggling. Lincoln faced increasing pressure from abolitionists and Republican politicians to free the slaves. Still, he also wanted to prevent the states that allowed slavery but were loyal to the Union from seceding and joining the Confederacy.

Lincoln bided his time, waiting for the perfect moment, and his patience paid off. The Union Army gained a major victory at the Battle of Antietam in Maryland, and it gave Lincoln the opportunity to issue an ultimatum to the Confederate States. He carefully crafted the Emancipation Proclamation, which allowed the border states within the Union to maintain their slaves but gave the Confederate states one hundred days to return to the Union. If they did not, their slaves would be declared free.

DECISION

The Emancipation Proclamation was an executive order issued by Lincoln declaring "all persons held as slaves within any State or designated part of a State, the people whereof shall then be in rebellion against the United States, shall be then, thenceforward, and forever free."

IMPACT

The Emancipation Proclamation was perhaps the most revolutionary measure an American president had ever taken up to that time. It profoundly changed the direction and outcome of the Civil War and American society in general, and it ultimately abolished the institution of slavery in the United States.

The decision to issue the Emancipation Proclamation was not without risk. Lincoln faced pushback from conservative Republicans and Democrats who feared it would prolong the war. Lincoln, however, believed it to be a military and foreign policy priority to preserve the country.

The Emancipation Proclamation was politically and militarily important, as it paved the way for over 180,000 African Americans to join the Union Army, significantly strengthening the Union's military force.

It balanced the importance of keeping the border states in the Union with the liberation of slaves within Confederate states. Many slaves attempted to escape after the Emancipation Proclamation, knowing the Union military would defend their actions.

The Emancipation Proclamation also put European and other international powers in a difficult position, having to decide whether to support the federal government or the Confederacy. Supporting slavery was untenable to many European nations, as they had already abolished the practice. Their citizens would not support such a position on moral grounds.

Even though it did not completely abolish slavery at the time, the Emancipation Proclamation set the stage for the Thirteenth Amendment to the Constitution, which ended slavery completely in the United States.

The Emancipation Proclamation also precipitated Lincoln's assassination in April 1865.

ANDREW JOHNSON

SEVENTEENTH PRESIDENT
DEMOCRAT/NATIONAL UNITY TICKET
TERM: 1865–1869
YEAR OF THE DECISION: 1865

CIRCUMSTANCE

Following the assassination of President Abraham Lincoln in 1865, Andrew Johnson became the 17th President of the United States. Johnson, a lifelong Democrat, had run as Lincoln's vice president on a National Unity Ticket, which combined Republicans with Southerners who did not support slavery. Thus, this was a wartime alliance between Republicans and pro-Union Democrats. Initially, Johnson maintained the National Unity position, but later in his presidency, he returned to his foundation as a supporter of states' rights in the mold of Andrew Jackson.

As the lone US Senator from the South who remained loyal to the Union when his home state of Tennessee seceded, Johnson was popular with Northern Republicans. He was vilified in the South; his family was run out of Tennessee, and his property was destroyed.

His pro-Union stance got Lincoln's attention, and he was appointed Military Governor of Tennessee.

After gaining an exemption to the Emancipation Proclamation for Tennessee and realizing that it was an essential tool for ending the war, Johnson accepted the Proclamation. His high profile as the only pro-Union Southern Senator and support of some of Lincoln's policies encouraged Lincoln to select him as his vice-presidential in his 1864 reelection bid, even though he was an Andrew Jackson-style populist Democrat.

It was Johnson who served as the nation's chief executive immediately after the Civil War and through the early stages of Reconstruction.

DECISION

Johnson's most consequential decision as president was to be lenient with the former Confederate states in order to rapidly reintegrate them into the Union.

IMPACT

Johnson's decision to be lenient with the former Confederate states prompted him to provide presidential pardons or amnesty to individuals who swore an oath of loyalty to the Union. He allowed former Confederate states to draft new Constitutions and opposed legislation and Constitutional amendments geared toward defending the freedoms of the newly freed former slaves.

This approach had far-reaching consequences, including the return of prominent Confederate politicians to positions of power, enabling Southern states to enact "Black Codes" laws that severely restricted the freedoms and rights of former slaves, and creating political strife within the US government.

Johnson and the Democrats suffered a resounding defeat in the 1866 midterm elections. Republicans rejected Johnson's pro-Southern polices and pursued more progressive Reconstruction legislation, which Johnson vetoed. The 1866 Civil Rights Act was the first major piece of legislation to be made into law by overriding a presidential veto. This legislation gave US citizenship to African Americans and explicitly protected them from discrimination. Within a few months, the Fourteenth Amendment was ratified, declaring that no state could "deprive any person of life, liberty, or property, without due process of law."

In 1867, the Radical Republicans passed new, additional Reconstructionist legislation that included limits on presidential authority, preventing Johnson from firing Cabinet officials. Despite this new law, Johnson terminated Secretary of War Edwin M. Stanton. It was this decision that led to Johnson being the first sitting president to be impeached, although he was acquitted by a single vote in the Senate.

Primarily due to his policies of being lenient toward—and even supportive of—former Confederate states and restricting the rights of newly freed slaves, Johnson's presidency is widely regarded as a failure. He effectively blocked the progress of civil rights for African Americans and increased racial tensions. His policies allowed the return of the horrible pre-Civil War socioeconomic conditions for African Americans in the South, just without slavery, and prevented the reforms necessary to enable newly freed slaves to thrive in the US

Johnson sought a full term but lost the 1868 Democratic nomination for president.

ULYSSES S. GRANT

EIGHTEENTH PRESIDENT
REPUBLICAN PARTY
TERM: 1869–1877
YEAR OF THE DECISION: 1869

CIRCUMSTANCE

Grant was a former military officer in the US Army and served under Lincoln as the Commanding General of the Union forces during the Civil War, ultimately leading to the Union's victory in 1865.

After the failures of Andrew Johnson, Grant was elected president in the middle of Reconstruction. Johnson had promoted lenient policies toward former Confederate states, and his inaction on protecting the rights and freedom of the newly released slaves resulted in the Republicans gaining over twenty House and two Senate seats in the 1866 midterm elections.

Running on the Republican ticket, Grant won the presidential election and initiated a path toward federal protection of former slaves and Black Americans more generally by providing an ongoing military presence in the South and preventing former Confederate political leaders from gaining power. This was, in fact, the first election in which freed former slave men could vote, bolstering Grant's victory.

DECISION

As a Radical Republican and an abolitionist, Grant decided to take a very aggressive pro-civil rights stance, using all means available to the federal government to protect Black Americans from discrimination.

IMPACT

During Grant's presidency, he demonstrated commitment to the core Republican values of supporting minority rights that he had fought so ferociously for in the Civil War. He was not afraid of or concerned about using federal troops to squash the Ku Klux Klan and other groups that attempted to prevent Black Americans from freely participating in American society.

Perhaps his greatest accomplishment was the passage of the Fifteenth Amendment, for which he fought hard and expended a great amount of political capital. This amendment granted voting rights to citizens regardless of race or previous servitude, marking a significant expansion of civil rights. Grant appointed Black and Jewish Americans to prominent federal offices.

Importantly, under Grant, the US Department of Justice (DOJ) was created, with one of its initial—and ongoing—roles being to protect the rights of Black Americans during the Reconstruction Era, particularly by enforcing the Fourteenth and Fifteenth Amendments. The DOJ carried out this mission by prosecuting Ku Klux

Klan members who were violently opposed to Grant's Reconstructionist policies.

RUTHERFORD B. HAYES

NINETEENTH PRESIDENT
REPUBLICAN PARTY
TERM: 1877–1881
YEAR OF THE DECISION: 1877

CIRCUMSTANCE

After serving two and a half terms as governor of Ohio, Rutherford B. Hayes was elected the nineteenth president of the United States. It was a hotly contested election that lasted for months. The electoral votes of three states, Louisiana, South Carolina, and Florida, were uncertain, as two sets of electors were submitted for each state—one set for Hayes and another for Samuel J. Tilden, his Democratic challenger. Both sides claimed victory. Republicans challenged the results, charging Democrats with fraud and voter suppression of Black Americans in Florida, Louisiana, and South Carolina. The disputed election and its controversial resolution through the Electoral Commission were highly contentious.

In January 1877, a Congressional commission was established to resolve the conflict. This commission, comprising Republicans, Democrats, and Supreme Court justices, was established to investigate the matter and determine the winner. Hayes was awarded all the electoral votes from the three states and declared the winner. From the outset, Hayes stated that he would serve only one term as president.

When he took office, it had only been twenty years since the Civil War; Reconstruction was nearly complete. The economy was in rough shape following the Panic of 1873, which led to a depression. Hayes, a former major general, Congressman, and governor, and a staunch abolitionist, entered the White House with a reputation for honesty, dignity, and political moderation. As part of a compromise to secure his election, Hayes pledged to protect the rights of Black Americans in the South while also pulling back from some of Grant's more aggressive Reconstructionist positions. This included the removal of federal troops from the South.

Hayes also sought to install individuals in high-ranking government positions based not on political favors but rather on merit. He thought these measures would build a new Republican Party, with Southern leaders and businessmen favoring Hayes's conservative fiscal policies. They did support his financial approach; however, politically, they could not be seen as supporting the party of Reconstruction.

Despite the conciliatory tone Hayes set in his inaugural address, many Democrats considered his election illegitimate and referred to him as "RutherFraud." Hayes's efforts to protect the rights of Black voters, persuade the South to accept racial equality, and enforce civil rights laws were in vain, as the Democratic-led House of Representatives stymied his efforts and, in fact, attempted to reverse some of the gains made under the prior administration.

DECISION

Withdrawing federal troops from the South and ending Reconstruction was the most significant decision Hayes made as US president.

IMPACT

With federal troops gone, Southern Democrats were able to revert back to racist policies, as there was no enforcement mechanism in place to protect the civil rights of African Americans. This precipitated Jim Crow laws and racial segregation throughout the South. Voter suppression was also widespread through a variety of racially motivated tactics.

As states passed laws to restrict voting rights, the political participation of both Black Americans and many poor White Americans declined. Between 1890 and 1910, ten of the eleven former Confederate states passed new Constitutions or amendments. These new laws were designed to disenfranchise most Black people and tens of thousands of poor White people through a combination of poll taxes, literacy and comprehension tests, and residency and record-keeping requirements.

While Hayes attempted to introduce other important legislation, such as reform of the government's civil service, it is the withdrawal of troops from the South that stands out as his most consequential action, due to its lasting adverse impact on civil rights.

JAMES GARFIELD

TWENTIETH PRESIDENT REPUBLICAN
TERM: 1881
YEAR OF THE DECISION: 1881

CIRCUMSTANCE

Garfield was a nine-term Congressman from the state of Ohio and also a former general in the Union Army. Before being elected president, he was one of the leading Republicans in the House of Representatives.

Garfield fought corruption at all levels of government, especially in New York, where one particular US senator and local politicians had taken control of the New York Customs House. The Customs House was the principal port of entry into the United States at the time. Through a variety of political maneuvering, Garfield won control over this crucial federal Institution.

Garfield was not able to accomplish much more than that, though, as two hundred days into his administration, on July 2, 1881, an assassin shot him inside a Washington railway station. President Garfield was mortally wounded but survived until September of that year, when he finally succumbed to his wound.

DECISION

Garfield's most important decision as president was to assert presidential authority over patronage and appointments, challenging the corrupt power of political machines and bosses, especially at the US Customs House in New York.

IMPACT

This decision was significant as it represented a substantial shift in the balance of power between the executive and legislative branches of government, particularly in the realm of political appointments. It demonstrated Garfield's commitment to civil service reform and willingness to challenge entrenched political interests, even within his own party.

CHESTER ARTHUR

TWENTY-FIRST PRESIDENT
REPUBLICAN PARTY
TERM: 1881–1885
YEAR OF THE DECISION: 1883

CIRCUMSTANCE

In 1881, an assassin's bullet took the life of James Garfield, propelling Chester Arthur to the presidency.

Although considered an honorable and honest politician, Arthur was a former quartermaster of the New York Customs House and was very familiar with the political machine, and in fact perpetuated it by increasing its staffing. Arthur made hiring decisions based on party loyalty, rather than effectiveness as government employees. That said, once the staff was installed, he insisted on the honest administration of the institution.

When his predecessor sought to gain control over the New York Customs House by outmaneuvering his political opponent, Senator Roscoe Conkling, Arthur threw his support behind Conkling, and not the president.

Interestingly, after succeeding to the presidency, Arthur became more aristocratic and avoided involvement with the well-established political machinery. In fact, during his tenure, Congress passed the Pendleton Act in 1883. Thanks to this new law, a bipartisan Civil Service Commission was created, which made political assessments for potential officeholders illegal, and provided for a "classified system" that made some government positions available only through a new competitive process that required written exams. Notably, it forbade the removal of protected government workers from their jobs for political reasons.

President Arthur tried to lower tariffs, as the US government was running a large financial surplus. The Tariff Act of 1883 was a mix, raising some tariffs while lowering others, but Arthur signed it into law nonetheless.

Arthur also signed the first federal immigration law, making pauperism, criminality, and lunacy reasons for denial. Chinese immigrants were banned for ten years, which was eventually made permanent.

Arthur ran the presidency as if he were a dying man. In fact, he was. About a year after ascending to the presidency, Arthur learned that he had a fatal kidney disease. Even so, he ran again for president in 1884 but was not nominated.

DECISION

Chester Arthur's most important decision as president was signing the Pendleton Act, which regulated the civil service.

IMPACT

The Pendleton Act played a critical role in reforming the federal government's hiring practices and reducing political corruption. It ended a political patronage system known as the "Spoils System," which favored cronyism over merit. This led to a more efficient and professional federal government bureaucracy.

The Act required applicants for certain positions to complete competitive examinations to be considered for a job, thereby improving the workforce. The Act also protected civil service workers from being removed from their jobs for political reasons.

Chester Arthur's support of the Pendleton Act was surprising, given his history as the quartermaster of the New York Customs House. His decision demonstrated that he ultimately valued good governance over party interests. This decision helped improve Arthur's reputation and demonstrated his independence from party pressure.

GROVER CLEVELAND

TWENTY-SECOND PRESIDENT
REPUBLICAN PARTY
TERM: 1885–1889
YEAR OF THE DECISION: 1886

CIRCUMSTANCE

In post-Civil War America, Republicans controlled the White House until Grover Cleveland was elected to the presidency through the combined support of Democrats and a group of Republican reformists, nicknamed the "Mugwumps." He was a hard worker, idealistic, and with an excellent memory.

Cleveland entered the White House a bachelor but married the daughter of his former law partner, thus becoming the first and only president to marry while in office. He was also the first president to be elected to nonconsecutive terms of office.

Cleveland presided over the dedication of the Statue of Liberty and saw the end of the Apache Wars with Geronimo's surrender. The Apache Wars were an almost-twenty-year period of armed conflict between the various Apache tribal confederations and the US military in the Southwest. The Apache Wars were part of the greater American Indian Wars and resulted from the expansion of American settlers into Apache lands.

As president, Cleveland was a staunch opponent of political corruption and fought vigorously to uphold the integrity of the offices in which he served. He was opposed to subsidies and special interests, which is why he used the veto a record-breaking 584 times—more than double the number of vetoes by all previous presidents. He was a strong monitor of Congress, which earned him the nickname the "Guardian President."

Cleveland pursued policies that barred special favors to any economic group. For example, he vetoed a bill to appropriate $10,000 to distribute seed grain among drought-stricken farmers in Texas. He wrote, "Federal aid in such cases encourages the expectation of paternal care on the part of the Government and weakens the sturdiness of our national character." Cleveland believed that hardship built character.

He ordered an investigation of western lands controlled by the railroad companies that they had obtained through government grants. He then drew their ire by forcing them to return 81,000,000 acres. Significantly, he signed the Interstate Commerce Act, the first law attempting to impose federal regulation on the railroads.

In general, he was not in favor of American imperialism nor the imperial moves of foreign powers.

At the end of 1885, Cleveland's vice president, Thomas Hendricks, died in office less than a year into his term. As a result, Cleveland was concerned about the line of succession in the event that anything was to befall the president and/or the vice president. Cleveland called for a Constitutional amendment to clarify and codify a line of succession.

DECISION

Cleveland's most important decision in his first term as president was to sign the Presidential Succession Act.

IMPACT

The Presidential Succession Act was important because it established the line of succession if both the president and vice president were unable to serve. It changed the previous legislation from 1792 by placing the heads of executive departments in line for the presidency after the vice president in the order in which the departments were created. It provided a long list of successors, making it practically impossible for the country to be without a head of state.

This Act remained in force until 1947, when it was superseded by a new succession plan.

BENJAMIN HARRISON

TWENTY-THIRD PRESIDENT
REPUBLICAN PARTY
TERM: 1889–1893
YEAR OF THE DECISION: 1890

CIRCUMSTANCE

Benjamin Harrison lost the popular vote but defeated Grover Cleveland in the Electoral College to become the nation's thirty-third president. He was a grandson of the ninth president, William Henry Harrison, and a great-grandson of Benjamin Harrison V, one of the Founding Fathers from Virginia who signed the Declaration of Independence. He served in the Union Army as a colonel and was confirmed by the Senate as a brevet brigadier general of volunteers. He served in the Senate from 1881 through 1887.

Three important areas of legislation during the Harrison administration included the McKinley Tariff, which imposed historic protective trade tariffs; the Sherman Antitrust Act; and the creation of the national forest reserves through an amendment to the Land Revision Act of 1891. Six western states were added to the nation while Harrison held office.

While strengthening and modernizing the Navy, he conducted an active foreign policy. He improved relations with Central and South American countries and sought to improve America's standing on the global stage. However, his domestic proposals to secure federal education funding and voting rights enforcement for African Americans were unsuccessful.

DECISION

The decision to sign the Sherman Antitrust Act into law was Benjamin Harrison's most important decision.

IMPACT

For the first time, federal law regulated trusts and monopolies. It outlawed business practices that would restrict trade and commerce, anti-competitive tactics, and monopolies. The Act laid the foundation for future legislation and enforcement.

Although it was rarely utilized during his administration, the Sherman Antitrust Act set a vital precedent for regulating business practices that would be used extensively by later administrations to combat anti-competitive practices and break up monopolistic corporations.

To this day, the Sherman Antitrust Act remains the foundation of American antitrust policies, providing the fundamental principles for legal enforcement and prosecution of offenders.

GROVER CLEVELAND

TWENTY-FOURTH PRESIDENT
DEMOCRATIC PARTY
TERM: 1893–1897
YEAR OF THE DECISION: 1893

CIRCUMSTANCE

Following the passage of the McKinley Tariff Act, the Republican administration embarked on a spending spree, depleting all of the government's surplus reserves. Cleveland easily beat his predecessor, Benjamin Harrison, to regain the presidency. An economic depression occurred early on in his second term, and Cleveland believed the depression was primarily due to a legal requirement that the US Treasury purchase 4.5 million ounces of silver each month. Cleveland called for a special session of Congress to repeal the requirement; however, his belief that this would resolve the country's economic woes was incorrect. The depression worsened.

Cleveland followed an economic course of action, backing paper currency with gold. His attitude that the government could do little more to alleviate economic suffering led to low morale in the country. His unpopular position worsened when he negotiated a deal with JP Morgan to sell government bonds abroad in order to replenish the Treasury's gold supply. This measure actually worked, but the venture with a despised "robber baron" further reduced Cleveland's popularity. He was perceived as losing touch with the common man.

In 1894, there was a widespread strike and boycott of the Pullman Railroad Company in Chicago. Cleveland's decision to send in federal troops to break the strike at the company's facility demonstrated his support of big business over the common laborer. He did this despite the governor of Illinois asking him not to. The strike was over within a week, and Cleveland was viewed favorably by business, but he had lost credibility with labor. It was during this labor action that, for the first time, an injunction was utilized to break a strike. On June 28, President Cleveland and Congress created a national holiday, Labor Day, as a conciliatory gesture toward American labor.

Cleveland demonstrated the same general principles in foreign policy that characterized much of his domestic policy. When he learned that the Hawaiian leader, Queen Liliuokalani, had been overthrown by an American-led coup, he withdrew a treaty for the annexation of Hawaii that his predecessor had submitted to the Senate for approval. He refused to intervene on behalf of Cuban insurgents fighting for independence from Spain. By invoking the Monroe Doctrine, he compelled Britain to accept arbitration of a boundary dispute between its colony of British Guiana, now Guyana, and its neighbor, Venezuela.

DECISION

Cleveland's decision to directly address the country's economic crisis by focusing on the US Treasury, rather than on unemployment and business failures, by maintaining the gold standard, was his most important and defining decision in his second term as president.

IMPACT

Cleveland firmly rejected the government's buildup of silver reserves in favor of maintaining, supporting, and strengthening the gold standard. He did this by authorizing multiple bond sales, which restored the gold reserves to a safe level.

Many Democrats supported the "Free Silver" policies, but Cleveland opposed them, and his position ultimately cost him the Democratic nomination for a third term.

The decision was controversial but critical in addressing the economic crisis and shaping future monetary policy. His actions also had lasting economic and political ramifications. The US continued with the gold standard until 1971, when Nixon decoupled the dollar from gold.

WILLIAM MCKINLEY

TWENTY-FIFTH PRESIDENT
REPUBLICAN PARTY
TERM: 1897–1901
YEAR OF THE DECISION: 1898

CIRCUMSTANCE

Prior to becoming president of the United States, William McKinley spent fourteen years in the House of Representatives and became the leading expert on tariffs. He then served two terms as governor of Ohio. He came into the presidency at the tail end of the economic depression that had dogged his predecessor, Grover Cleveland.

Foreign policy dominated McKinley's presidency. Despite his position of "neutral intervention," in 1898, he effectively declared war on Spain, which was battling revolutionaries in Cuba. Widespread reports of large-scale Cuban fatalities and great suffering forced McKinley into a military solution.

On February 15, 1898, the USS Maine exploded and sank in Havana Harbor, escalating tensions between the US and Spain. As a result, McKinley asked Congress for a declaration of war, which officially started the Spanish-American War. US forces went on to destroy the Spanish Navy in Cuba and took control of Manila in the Philippines and Puerto Rico. The one-hundred-day war was a decisive victory for America.

Unsure of what to do with the captured territories, McKinley toured the nation to gauge public sentiment. The population called for territorialism, so McKinley officially annexed the territories, which included Puerto Rico, Guam, and the Philippines.

Shortly after winning a second term, McKinley was felled by an assassin's bullet and died eight days later.

DECISION

Although he initially resisted involvement, public pressure and the failure of diplomatic solutions led to McKinley's decision to use military force in the Spanish-Cuban conflict. This decision had far-reaching and long-term consequences for US foreign policy and played an essential role in the nation's emergence as a global power.

IMPACT

The destruction of the Spanish fleet within one hundred days demonstrated the power of the US Navy, positioning the nation as one of the most potent in the world. The capture and annexation of Spanish territories marked a major shift toward international territorialism for the United States. It transformed the US from a continental power to a global power with overseas possessions. Eventually, the US developed military bases in these territories, which proved vital in other wars.

McKinley was initially widely viewed as a weak president, but the Spanish-American War demonstrated his authority over his Cabinet and military advisors, which bolstered his reputation and legacy.

THEODORE ROOSEVELT

TWENTY-SIXTH PRESIDENT
REPUBLICAN PARTY
TERM: 1901–1909
YEAR OF THE DECISION: 1901

CIRCUMSTANCE

After McKinley was assassinated, Theodore Roosevelt became the US's youngest president at age forty-two. He brought to the country a new vigor, with aggressive and progressive ideas about both domestic and foreign policy.

Before entering politics, Roosevelt struggled with the loss of his wife and his mother on the same day. He took time to reflect on his life while spending almost two years in the Badlands of the Dakota Territory, living a rugged life in the saddle while hunting big game.

He was a war hero, leading the charge at the Battle of San Juan Hill in the Spanish-American War as a lieutenant colonel of the Rough Riders. Following the war, he successfully ran for governor of New York and did an admirable job in that position.

As president, he broadened the power of the chief executive by assuming the position that, as president, he was the "Steward of the People" and, unless specifically forbidden by law or the Constitution, he held the authority to pursue his agenda. An example of this was his passage of the Pure Food and Drug Act and the Meat Inspection Act in 1906, which established food safety regulations and served as the precursors to today's FDA.

Roosevelt believed that the government should help balance the opposing economic forces of labor and capitalist businesses. Accordingly, he used the Sherman Antitrust Act to successfully bust the great railroad corporations of the Northwest. More antitrust suits followed, earning him the nickname "Trust-Buster."

With respect to world politics, his philosophy was guided by his famous maxim, "Speak softly but carry a big stick." Recognizing the need to connect the Atlantic and Pacific Oceans, his administration initiated the construction of the Panama Canal. Roosevelt disallowed the development and establishment of foreign bases in the Caribbean by adding his own corollary to the Monroe Doctrine, further establishing the US's sole right to prevent foreign interference in all of Latin America. He sent the "Great White Fleet" on a world tour to demonstrate American naval power and was awarded the Nobel Peace Prize for negotiating an end to the Russo-Japanese War.

Sparked by his time in the Dakotas, Roosevelt was a pioneer in protecting and conserving the environment. Under his presidency, 150 national forests, 51 federal bird reserves, 4 national game preserves, 5 national parks, and 18 national monuments were established, protecting approximately 230 million acres of public land.

DECISION

Roosevelt decided to aggressively exert executive power to manage and protect the country's wilderness and environment, which he believed was critical for future generations. From his perspective, the government had the great responsibility to use the nation's natural resources responsibly and wisely.

IMPACT

Roosevelt's environmental policies have had a long-lasting impact on American environmental policy and public lands. It established his legacy as a great environmental preservationist. His policies established precedents for federal stewardship of natural resources, which continue to impact decisions about land use and environmental protection today. His aggressive posture resulted in major expansions of federal authority and helped make conservation a national priority.

WILLIAM HOWARD TAFT

TWENTY-SEVENTH PRESIDENT
REPUBLICAN PARTY
TERM: 1909–1913
YEAR OF THE DECISION: 1911

CIRCUMSTANCE

Fathered by a distinguished judge, Taft graduated from Yale, then studied and practiced law in Cincinnati. He preferred law to politics and was appointed a federal circuit judge at age thirty-four. He dreamed of becoming a member of the Supreme Court, but his wife, Helen, had political aspirations for him.

Taft spent time in the Philippines as the Chief Civil Administrator appointed by President McKinley. Excelling in this position, he improved the local infrastructure, schools, and economy. He even allowed limited participation in government by Filipinos. Roosevelt had appointed Taft his Secretary of War and designated him as his successor as president.

Once he became president, Taft committed to following Roosevelt's policies, although the strong-arm tactics that his predecessor employed were not in his toolbox. He maintained high tariffs, which alienated liberal Republicans so much that they broke off into the Progressive Party.

His administration initiated eighty antitrust suits, including a major case against US Steel. He got legislation approved to establish a federal income tax and the direct election of Senators. These actions, however, received little attention, as all the noise centered on tariffs and the economy.

The Sixteenth Amendment gave Congress the power to levy income taxes without apportioning them among the states. It was championed by President Taft and ratified in 1913.

The Republican Party nominated Taft for reelection; however, Roosevelt left the party to run with the Progressives, which opened the door for Democrat Woodrow Wilson to win the presidency. Several years later, President Harding appointed Taft to the esteemed position of Chief Justice of the Supreme Court of the United States, the dream job he sought when he was much younger, becoming the only person to hold both the presidency and the head of the American judicial system.

DECISION

The decision to very aggressively enforce antitrust laws and create a fair and competitive economy was Taft's most important decision as US president.

IMPACT

Taft's targeting of perhaps the largest US corporation at the time, US Steel, demonstrated that no company was too big to avoid prosecution for monopolistic practices.

This sent a powerful message to other large corporations.

In the legal filings, Taft asserted that Roosevelt had erred in allowing US Steel to purchase the Tennessee Coal and Iron Company in 1907. This severely damaged the relationship between Taft and Roosevelt.

Taft's approach set the stage for the enforcement of antitrust regulations throughout the twentieth century. It proved his commitment to the rule of law by taking on the largest corporations.

WOODROW WILSON

TWENTY-EIGHTH PRESIDENT
DEMOCRATIC PARTY
TERM: 1913–1921
YEAR OF THE DECISION: 1917

CIRCUMSTANCE

Woodrow Wilson was elected during a time of peace in the United States. A lawyer and academic with a PhD in political science, Wilson became the president of Princeton University. Democratic insiders saw Wilson's potential as presidential material and persuaded him to run for and become governor of New Jersey, a stepping stone toward the US presidency.

The country was in the midst of progressive reform and social activism when Wilson was elected to the presidency. His predecessors had taken sharp aim at large monopolistic corporations. The US was emerging as a global power, yet it remained largely an isolationist nation. There was a large wave of immigration from Southern and Eastern Europe, sparking concerns about immigration policy. Tariffs were the primary source of federal income, as there were no personal or corporate income taxes.

During the election of 1912, the Republicans imploded and split off into two main factions: traditional Republicans with Taft and Progressives who supported Roosevelt. The division of the Republican vote provided an opening for the Democrat, Wilson, to obtain the presidency.

As president, Wilson accomplished a great many things both domestically and in foreign policy. Among them, he established the Federal Reserve System, which provided a stable monetary and financial system for the federal government, and the Federal Trade Commission to prevent unfair business practices. He enacted laws prohibiting child labor.

Under Wilson, the Women's Suffrage Movement gained momentum, and the Nineteenth Amendment, granting women the right to vote, was ratified.

While he maintained neutrality in World War I during his first term in office, Wilson ultimately brought the United States into the war with the call to "Make the world safe for democracy." This provided critical support and turned the tide in favor of the Allies.

Wilson had a clear vision for a post-war world. He laid this out in his Fourteen Points speech, which included principles such as self-determination, free trade, disarmament, and the establishment of a League of Nations to ensure collective security and peace.

Toward the end of his presidency, the nation was turning toward Republicanism once again, and Wilson could not get Congressional support to join the League of Nations, the precursor of what is now the United Nations.

In October 1919, Wilson suffered a severe, near-fatal

stroke, which left him paralyzed on his left side, nearly blind in both eyes, and speechless. His condition was hidden from the American people and Congress. His wife, Edith, acted as a go-between, with only herself and his physician allowed to see the president. Unbeknownst to the rest of the world, Edith assumed many of the president's responsibilities. Wilson's condition likely contributed to the country's decision not to join the League of Nations, as it hindered his ability to directly persuade Congressional leadership. Wilson partially recovered from the effects of his stroke, but never fully regained his mental and physical status.

DECISION

While achieving many legislative victories on the domestic front, Wilson's most important decision was to enter World War I by signing the Declaration of War against Germany.

IMPACT

Entering World War I had several highly significant ramifications. First, it shifted the balance of power in favor of the Allies. The slogan "Make the world safe for democracy" was both a rallying cry and a foreign policy statement that has guided US political thought through the twentieth century and beyond. Economically, it resulted in a massive mobilization of American resources, a military draft, increased taxation, and government control over various sectors of the economy.

The US's involvement and leadership in World War I set the stage for America to become a global superpower in the twentieth century.

WARREN G. HARDING

TWENTY-NINTH PRESIDENT
REPUBLICAN PARTY
TERM: 1921–1923
YEAR OF THE DECISION: 1921

CIRCUMSTANCE

A good-natured newspaperman from Ohio, Warren Harding first ascended the political ladder in his state legislature, where he served two terms. This was followed by a stint as lieutenant governor. After that, he returned to the newspaper business. Four years later, he won a seat in the US Senate. Harding was a conservative Republican who supported the interests of business and protective tariffs. As a Republican, he opposed Wilson's post-war plans and supported the prohibition of alcohol. He ran promising "a return to normalcy."

Harding was well-known to Republican leaders and did not have any notable political enemies. As a staunch Republican, he was "right" on all the issues and represented the critically important state of Ohio. During the Republican National Convention of 1920, the nomination was deadlocked after ten rounds of voting.

Harding emerged as the nominee, with Calvin Coolidge his choice for vice-president, on the eleventh ballot. He handily won the election, becoming the first US senator to do so.

Determined to turn back the momentum of the Progressive Movement, he used his authority as president to personally overturn or allow Congress to reverse many policies of the Wilson Administration. He supported limiting immigration and gave tax cuts to wealthy Americans. He signed the Unified Budget Act, which allowed the president to submit a single budget to Congress instead of individual departmental budgets. Harding created the General Accounting Office to audit government expenditures.

Harding was a champion of civil rights for Black Americans and created the Veterans' Bureau, which coordinated the medical care of World War I veterans.

On the foreign policy front, his administration helped elevate American banking to a global position and negotiated trade deals to acquire rubber in British Malaya and oil in the Middle East. Harding also played an essential role in rebuilding Europe after World War I and established an "open door" trading policy in Asia.

While attempting to fulfill his promise of hiring the "best man for the job," he did the opposite by awarding important government positions to his political supporters. Some of his appointees were highly effective; however, other high-level appointees, known as the "Ohio Gang," proved to be unscrupulous and corrupt, leading to a scandal. The worst, known as the "Teapot Dome" scandal, resulted in the Secretary of the Interior being imprisoned for leasing oil-rich government lands in Wyoming in return for personal loans. Additionally, his attorney general faced two impeachments and two indictments, causing him to resign during Coolidge's administration.

On August 2, 1923, Harding had a massive, unexpected, fatal heart attack while on a trip to California. He had been president for less than three years.

DECISION

It is challenging to select a single, defining decision that Warren G. Harding made as president as his most important. However, his decision early in his presidency to restore the country to normalcy post-World War I was a theme that guided his administration. This meant a return to right-leaning Republican policies, was a decision of consequence for Harding.

IMPACT

The "return to normalcy" policies of the Harding administration mainly were domestic and included such actions as reducing federal government expenditures to lower the tax burden on citizens. To curb inflation, he encouraged the Federal Reserve Board to cut the money supply.

Marking a deviation from both Wilson and Roosevelt, Harding's administration was more business-friendly. He supported the rapid downsizing of the military after its buildup during World War I.

In response to growing nativism, he restricted immigration through the Emergency Quota Act.

With respect to foreign policy, he supported American isolationism and opposed US entry into the League of

Nations. He also encouraged diplomacy to decrease international tensions, as exemplified by his approval of the Washington Naval Conference of 1921–1922 to limit international naval armaments.

These policies had mixed results overall, but they certainly helped bring the country from a wartime mentality and economy to a more stable peacetime situation.

CALVIN COOLIDGE

THIRTIETH PRESIDENT REPUBLICAN
TERM: 1923–1929
YEAR OF THE DECISION: 1923

CIRCUMSTANCE

On August 2, 1923, following the sudden death of President Harding, Calvin Coolidge received word by messenger that he was the new president. His father, whom he was visiting at their family home in Vermont, was a village shopkeeper and a notary public who administered the Oath of Office. Coolidge placed his hand on the family Bible and was sworn in by the light of a kerosene lantern, as there was no electricity in the house.

Before becoming Harding's vice president, Coolidge studied law and became the governor of Massachusetts. He was a Republican and very conservative.

As the post-World War I economy continued to improve, Coolidge's popularity increased. His primary goal as president was to maintain the status quo. He achieved this goal by basically doing nothing. For example, he vetoed bills that would aid farmers and also a bill to provide inexpensive electricity to the Tennessee

Valley. He was a man of few words, frequently simply giving "Yes" or "No" answers without explanations. However, on a personal level, he was a kind and approachable president.

At the time he became president, the country was still embroiled in the political corruption scandals of the Harding administration. The death of Harding created considerable uncertainty in the political world, and the country needed guidance to restore stability and confidence in the federal government.

In December 1923, Coolidge became the first president to deliver a nationwide radio address to the country. Technical advances, such as broadcast radio, affordable automobiles (thanks to the advent of the assembly line), movies with sound, aviation, and improved household appliances, all contributed to economic growth and led to the "Roaring Twenties." This was one of the most prosperous times in American history.

Socially, Prohibition was in effect, and women gaining the right to vote yielded political influence unseen in the past. Urbanization and modernization were advancing rapidly. The Ku Klux Klan was resurging as well, and Coolidge refused to nominate any members for office, as he was a supporter of civil rights. Similarly, Coolidge signed the Indian Citizenship Act in 1924, granting full citizenship to all Native Americans while allowing them to retain tribal land rights.

He was the Republican nominee for president in 1924 and cruised to victory with over 2.5 million more votes than his two opponents.

In 1927, during a trip to South Dakota, the man of few words famously and simply stated, "I do not choose to run for president in 1928."

DECISION

Adopting a policy of fiscal conservatism and tax reductions was the cornerstone decision that Coolidge made early in his presidency.

IMPACT

Passage of the Revenue Act of 1926 substantially reduced federal income taxes. This decision was in accordance with Coolidge's philosophy that smaller government and lower taxes were key to economic prosperity. His fiscal policies balanced the federal budget and eliminated the national debt, making the country a surplus nation.

His hands-off approach was consistent with his conservative values. He demonstrated his commitment to limited government by not intervening in the depressed agricultural industry, as evidenced by his veto of two farm relief bills. Some blame Coolidge's laissez-faire ideology for contributing to the Great Depression that broke out under his successor.

Coolidge is often misquoted as saying, "The business of America is business." His actual quote was a bit more elaborate: "After all, the business of the American people is business. They are profoundly concerned with producing, buying, selling, investing, and prospering in the world." In the same speech, he went on to say that Americans want more, including "peace and honor and charity, which is so strong an element of all civilization." Thus, the words of "Silent Cal" were made even shorter and frequently misquoted throughout the years.

HERBERT HOOVER

THIRTY-FIRST PRESIDENT
REPUBLICAN PARTY
TERM: 1929–1933
YEAR OF THE DECISION: 1930

CIRCUMSTANCE

When Hoover was elected president, he benefited from the economic prosperity of his predecessors. Hoover had been Secretary of Commerce under both and campaigned on continuing their fiscal policies.

Hoover was also known as "The Great Humanitarian," having been the head of the American Relief Administration, which helped feed the hungry in war-torn Europe following World War I. When he extended aid to the famine-stricken Soviet Russia in 1921, a critic inquired if he was not thus helping Bolshevism. Hoover retorted, "Twenty million people are starving. Whatever their politics, they shall be fed!" He had also gained international recognition as a capable administrator and brilliant engineer, being the driving force behind what is now known as the Hoover Dam.

Many believed Hoover's election would end poverty

in the US, but the reality was very different. A few short months later, the stock market crashed, and the nation fell into the Great Depression. His proposed solution was to balance the federal budget while reducing taxes and expanding public works programs and spending. He asked business leaders not to cut wages and to retain employees. Although he had a positive reputation for feeding post-war Europe, he took a hands-off approach in the US, leaving that responsibility to voluntary organizations and local governments.

Hoover's approaches did not help the foundering economy, and he watched as businesses closed their doors and Americans sank into poverty. He also made a critical mistake in signing into law the Smoot-Hawley Act, which raised taxes on imports, prompting foreign nations to stop buying American products at a time when the US desperately needed such sales.

He became a scapegoat for the Depression and was severely defeated in the 1932 election.

DECISION

Hoover's decision to take indirect measures in response to the Great Depression, rather than direct federal support to individuals, contributed to the economy's downward spiral.

IMPACT

Hoover believed in supporting state committees and encouraging volunteerism, rather than providing direct federal assistance to individuals. His insistence on keeping a balanced federal budget meant that government intervention would be limited. However, the scope of the Great Depression was so broad that such limited measures were ineffective. Hoover did not implement any major federal programs, such as adjusting the value of the dollar, price fixing, or putting controls on business, as he thought these actions would lead to socialism.

Hoover's policies shaped the public perception of him as uncaring toward everyday Americans, despite his earlier reputation for humanitarian work.

FRANKLIN DELANO ROOSEVELT

THIRTY-SECOND PRESIDENT
DEMOCRATIC PARTY
TERM: 1933–1945
YEAR OF THE DECISION: 1941

CIRCUMSTANCE

Having been elected to four terms in office, Franklin Delano Roosevelt (FDR) was America's longest-serving president. An entire generation grew up knowing no other president than FDR.

Roosevelt attended Harvard University and Columbia Law School, although he left Columbia early without graduating because he had passed the bar exam. President Wilson appointed him Assistant Secretary of the Navy, the same job his fifth cousin, Theodore Roosevelt, had used to catapult himself to the presidency. In 1914, FDR ran for Senate, but learned a valuable lesson: even though he had national stature, he could not win against a well-organized local political organization. In 1920, he was the Democratic nominee for vice president on a losing ticket.

In 1921, at the age of thirty-nine, Roosevelt contracted polio, which left him in wheelchair and crutches. Despite desperate efforts, he never regained the use of his legs.

When FDR first ran for president, the country was in the middle of the Great Depression. Thirteen million people were unemployed, and almost every bank had closed. Republicans were being blamed for the Great Depression. Sensing an opportunity, Roosevelt began his run for the presidency by calling for the government to provide relief, recovery, and reform. He was elected handily, and in his inaugural address, he famously told the country, "The only thing we have to fear is fear itself."

Just eight days after he became president, FDR initiated his series of live "Fireside Chats" from the White House, where he addressed the nation via radio. The first explained the banking problem and the government's response to it. These folksy speeches were a powerful tactic to gain American support for his New Deal policies.

FDR made dramatic changes to the government's approach to the economy. He took the nation off the gold standard and ran fiscal deficits. He created Social Security and placed higher taxes on the wealthy. He temporarily closed all the banks to prevent runs on deposits, created an insurance program for bank deposits, and eventually put new controls on banks and public utilities. He initiated enormous work-relief programs for the unemployed. Thus, he implemented both systemic and individualized initiatives to boost the economy. He labeled these policies and reforms the New Deal.

In 1936, he was reelected by a wide margin and believed he had a popular mandate to continue his policies. He sought legislation to enlarge the Supreme Court, which had been invalidating key New Deal measures, but he was unsuccessful.

In foreign policy, he made a concerted effort to keep the US out of the escalating war in Europe. He passed neutrality legislation, yet also tried to strengthen allied nations, which were either under threat from or actively at war with Germany. When France fell and Britain came under siege in 1940, he began to send Great Britain all possible aid short of actual military involvement through a program called the Lend-Lease Act. America had held an isolationist policy in foreign affairs since 1918, when World War I concluded. In the early 1930s, Congress passed the Neutrality Acts to prevent the United States from becoming entangled in foreign conflicts. As he was prohibited by law from providing assets to support the Allied war efforts, FDR got around these laws on a technicality by leasing equipment to them.

With German victories in Europe and Japan's growing dominance in Asia, FDR believed that only he possessed the experience and skills to lead America through the challenging times ahead. With that in mind, he ran for a third term and was elected.

As Americans learned more about the war atrocities, isolationist attitudes diminished. Then, the Japanese sneak attack on Pearl Harbor on December 7, 1941, changed the dynamics of world events. Roosevelt readied the country's military forces and resources for global warfare.

Roosevelt, his generals, and the Allies developed a

strategy for defeating Germany through a series of invasions, first in North Africa in 1942, then in Sicily and Italy in 1943, and then the large-scale D-Day invasion of Europe in 1944. Allied forces also pushed back Japan in Asia and the eastern Pacific. Roosevelt promoted the concept of a United Nations as it became clear that relations between the US and the Soviet Union needed strengthening.

During the war, Roosevelt signed an executive order stating that all persons of Japanese descent must vacate the West Coast, resulting in 120,000 people—many of them American citizens—being sent to internment camps located inland. Strangely enough, in Hawaii, where one-third of the population was of Japanese descent, there was no such order. Likewise, Americans of Italian or German ancestry were not interned.

There was little doubt that FDR would run for an unprecedented fourth term, as the US was still deeply involved in World War II. Roosevelt selected Senator Harry S. Truman from Missouri to be his vice-presidential running mate, and they defeated Republican Thomas E. Dewey in the 1944 election, carrying thirty-six of the forty-eight states.

Throughout his presidency, Roosevelt's wife, Eleanor, also had a larger-than-life reputation with the American public. Outspoken on issues such as civil rights, women's rights, the underprivileged, and basic human rights, she transformed the role of the First Lady.

Roosevelt's health deteriorated toward the end of the war, and on April 12, 1945, he died of a cerebral hemorrhage. FDR's sudden death shook America to its core.

DECISION

FDR made many immensely important decisions during his presidency, but his most important decision was to bring the United States into World War II after the Japanese attack on Pearl Harbor in December 1941.

IMPACT

The decision to enter World War II had far-reaching consequences well beyond the shores of the United States. His New Deal policies and programs were hugely successful in combating the Great Depression and reshaping American society, but entering the war had a profound and long-lasting impact.

This decision turned the tide of the war, unleashing the strength of the US military against the Axis powers of Germany, Italy, and Japan. By making this decision, Roosevelt turned the US into a global superpower with great responsibilities and influence over nations.

As part of its military expansion, the US won the nuclear race thanks to the Manhattan Project, ushering in the atomic age.

FDR's concept of a United Nations organization came to fruition after the war, and his leadership established America as the leader of the "Free World" dedicated to freedom and democracy. This position would dominate US foreign policy going forward.

HARRY S. TRUMAN

THIRTY-THIRD PRESIDENT
DEMOCRATIC PARTY
TERM: 1933–1945
YEAR OF THE DECISION: 1945

CIRCUMSTANCE

In January 1945, FDR was inaugurated for the fourth time, and in April of that year, he passed away. His compromise vice president, Harry S. Truman, inherited the presidency at a critical moment. World War II was winding down in Europe, but Asia was still a challenge. Thus, Truman faced tremendous challenges both at home and in foreign policy.

Truman grew up in Independence, Missouri, and had worked on the family farm. He served in World War I and, upon his return, went into local politics. Truman had a reputation for honesty, integrity, and fighting political corruption. Truman was elected to the US Senate and headed the "Truman Committee," whose focus was on identifying and reducing waste and inefficiency in wartime contracts and spending. The Democratic machine viewed Truman as a better choice for FDR's vice president than his third-term VP, Henry Wallace.

When Truman assumed the presidency, World War II was nearing its end, yet the battle still raged on in Asia. It was estimated that to achieve a complete victory, America could lose one million troops—or more. The Japanese willingness to fight ferociously to the death was demonstrated at Iwo Jima and Okinawa, which raised concerns about what it would take to defeat Japan.

At home, Americans were becoming weary of war. The death toll was high, and the strain on their lifestyles was great, as the government implemented rationing of food items such as sugar, coffee, and meat, as well as gasoline. Perhaps even more importantly, many men were fighting abroad or stationed far away from their homes for extended periods. The human emotional impact was tremendous.

Truman had to make many decisions as both a wartime and peacetime president. His famous motto, which he enshrined on a plaque on his desk, was "The buck stops here."

Later in his presidency, Truman took decisive action in dismissing the famous World War II general Douglas MacArthur for publicly disagreeing with him on policy decisions related to the Korean War. MacArthur wanted to expand America's involvement in the Korean War by invading China and advocated the potential use of nuclear weapons in China. His comments were confusing to Americans and allies alike, leaving them wondering whether the military or the civilian government was in control. Truman made the highly unpopular decision to relieve the much-admired general of command after consulting with his senior advisors, including the heads of the military branches, who agreed. But this was not Truman's most consequential decision.

DECISION

Undoubtedly, the most critical decision Truman made—and perhaps the most difficult decision any US president has ever made—was to be the first country to use atomic weapons on an adversary, causing the immediate deaths of tens of thousands of civilians and the instant destruction of entire cities.

IMPACT

Many important considerations went into Truman's decision to use nuclear weapons on Japan. A major one was preventing the loss of one million American soldiers in a protracted war. This weighed heavily on Truman, as he had personally witnessed the death and destruction of World War I. Despite the use of tremendous conventional weaponry thus far, Japan refused to surrender.

The immense power of the nuclear bomb would deal a stunning blow to Japan, which Truman believed would result in Japan's rapid surrender and the conclusion of World War II. At the time, he saw little difference between utilizing the atomic bomb and conventional methods of warfare, such as firebombing Japanese cities.

Truman was also aware that by using the atomic bomb, the US would have vast influence and leverage over world affairs, particularly with the Soviets.

Interestingly, Truman rejected the idea of testing a bomb to demonstrate its power, hoping that Japan would surrender. Understanding the Japanese mindset steered Truman to drop the two atomic bombs without warning.

The impact of Truman's decision to drop atomic bombs on Hiroshima and Nagasaki was profound and multifaceted. It included immediate human devastation, long-term health effects, geopolitical shifts, and ethical debates that continue to this day.

Their use marked the start of the nuclear age, leading to an arms race during the Cold War. It gave the US a military superiority that other countries desired to curb.

Survivors of the bombings, known as hibakusha, faced long-term health consequences. The radiation caused leukemia, other cancers, and chronic illnesses. The psychological trauma and social stigma associated with being a hibakusha further compounded their suffering. The bombings also had intergenerational effects, increasing birth defects and genetic mutations in the children of hibakusha.

Ultimately, the use of atomic weapons caused Japan to surrender. In addition, the Truman Doctrine—which stated that the US was committed to supporting "free peoples" resisting subjugation by armed minorities or outside pressures—effectively expanded US foreign policy interests across the globe. Before this, the Monroe Doctrine had largely limited the US's foreign involvement to the Western Hemisphere.

Thus, the use of atomic weapons not only ended World War II but was also pivotal in reshaping global politics. It shaped society's understanding of the possibility of self-destruction and its view on the future use of nuclear weaponry.

DWIGHT D. EISENHOWER

THIRTY-FOURTH PRESIDENT
REPUBLICAN PARTY
TERM: 1953–1961
YEAR OF THE DECISION: 1957

CIRCUMSTANCE

Dwight David Eisenhower (popularly known as "Ike") was raised in Kansas and attended West Point Military Academy. Throughout the First World War, Ike was disappointed to be assigned to run a tank training center near Gettysburg, Pennsylvania, rather than being stationed overseas. Throughout World War I and thereafter, Eisenhower continued to rise through the ranks, working under some of the greatest US generals, and eventually achieved the highest military position.

In 1941, Eisenhower was transferred to the War Plans Division in Washington, DC, where he was promoted to major general. Soon after, he was named commander in chief of the Allied Forces and led Operation Torch, the Allied invasion of North Africa. Eisenhower was concerned that diverting military resources would adversely impact the war effort in Europe.

On D-Day, June 6, 1944, Eisenhower commanded the Allied forces, having virtually invented the concept of an Allied unified command and persuaded the British to accept it in lieu of their committee system. In December 1944, he was promoted to the rank of five-star general.

Following World War II, Eisenhower returned home to Kansas to a hero's welcome. Just a few months later, he was made US Army Chief of Staff. After he left the military, he became president of Columbia University in 1948. In 1950, he left Columbia to accept an appointment as the first Supreme Allied Commander of the North Atlantic Treaty Organization (NATO).

Eisenhower was so popular that both the Democrats and Republicans recruited him to be their presidential nominee. As the Republican nominee, he won a landslide victory in 1952. His slogan was the simple, yet catchy, "I like Ike."

The conflict on the Korean Peninsula was heating up, and Eisenhower was so worried about it that he made it a substantial campaign issue. He even committed to going there personally to see the situation firsthand. He fulfilled his promise by going to South Korea as president-elect, and his experiences guided his decisions as president.

By 1953, the Korean War had been ongoing for nearly three years and had reached a stalemate. US citizens were tired of the conflict and wanted an honorable resolution. Within six months of entering office, Eisenhower successfully negotiated the Korean Armistice Agreement, which provided for South Korean security and allowed many US troops to return home.

His domestic agenda largely followed those of Roosevelt and Truman, continuing with most New Deal policies while also emphasizing a balanced budget. A strong civil rights advocate, he enforced desegregation of schools by sending troops into Little Rock, Arkansas, to assure compliance with federal court orders. He also ordered the complete desegregation of the Armed Forces, saying, "There must be no second-class citizens in this country."

Eisenhower was keenly interested in reducing the likelihood of nuclear war. He initiated the Atoms for Peace program in a speech at the United Nations General Assembly, which advocated for the peaceful use of atomic energy. Recognizing the destructive power of the hydrogen bomb—which both the US and the Soviet Union had developed—he met with Soviet, British, and French leaders in Geneva to further prevent the threat of atomic war. While uncommitted, the Soviets were somber and appreciative of the approach.

Ike won a second term in office. During his presidency, Alaska and Hawaii were admitted as states. Notably, he supported the establishment of the Interstate Highway System. Other important decisions included signing the 1957 Civil Rights Act and setting up a permanent Civil Rights Commission. Eisenhower is credited with establishing the National Aeronautics and Space Administration (NASA).

DECISION

In the pivotal Brown v. Board of Education case of 1954, the Supreme Court decided that segregated schools were unconstitutional. When the Arkansas governor defied a federal court order to integrate Little Rock Central

High School in 1957, Eisenhower intervened.

He mobilized the Arkansas National Guard and deployed troops from the 101st Airborne Division to ensure the safety of the Black students attempting to enroll at the school. This action marked a pivotal moment in the Civil Rights Movement and was Eisenhower's most crucial decision as president.

IMPACT

The consequences of Eisenhower's decision during the Little Rock Crisis were significant and far-reaching, as it affirmed federal authority to enforce Supreme Court rulings, particularly in matters of civil rights and desegregation. The message was clear: the federal government would support and enforce integration.

While earlier administrations were reluctant to intervene in the issue of segregation, Eisenhower symbolized the federal government's commitment to upholding civil rights and protecting the rights of African American citizens.

This also set a legal precedent for future civil rights cases. It established that federal courts and the executive branch could use federal troops to enforce desegregation orders. This became a critical tool in advancing civil rights in the US.

The Little Rock Crisis had a profound impact on both politics and society, garnering national and international attention and highlighting the issue of segregation in America. It fueled public discussions and generated support for additional civil rights legislation. It influenced future presidents and their policies toward civil rights and the role of the federal government.

JOHN F. KENNEDY

THIRTY-FIFTH PRESIDENT
DEMOCRATIC PARTY
TERM: 1961–1963
YEAR OF THE DECISION: 1962

CIRCUMSTANCE

The domestic and international social, economic, and political environments leading up to the election of 1960 were complex. The sitting vice president, Richard Nixon, faced Democratic nominee John Fitzgerald Kennedy (JFK), a young senator from Massachusetts with a charismatic appeal. His innovative use of television, including the first televised presidential debate, played a significant role in shaping the public's perception of the candidates. Kennedy's Catholic faith was a contentious issue, but he addressed it effectively, advocating for the absolute separation of church and state.

Kennedy, who came from a wealthy Massachusetts family, was practically raised to be president. His father already had a strong political foundation, along with the financial resources to help fund his son's political career and presidential campaign. His father had also served as the US Ambassador to Britain, which provided JFK with valuable political experience. The family's political aspirations for their sons were substantial, and they actively pushed them toward political careers, with the ultimate goal of one or more of them reaching the presidency. They had an instinctive ability to leverage media attention, which played a decisive role in JFK's campaign.

JFK served as a lieutenant on patrol boat PT-109 in World War II. The boat was rammed and sliced in half by the Japanese destroyer Amagiri, killing two crew members instantly. Kennedy and ten other survivors clung to the wreckage throughout the night. His bravery was apparent when he towed an injured crewman three miles to a small island, swimming with the man's life jacket strap between his teeth. For six days, JFK repeatedly swam into dangerous waters, trying to signal for help. Kennedy and his crew were finally rescued with the help of Solomon Islander scouts and an Australian Coastwatcher. He received the Navy and Marine Corps Medal for his heroic actions during this incident, which made him a genuine war hero.

Civil rights, an ongoing issue in America, proved to be an asset for JFK. When Martin Luther King, Jr., was arrested, Kennedy intervened and secured his release, which led to increased support from Black voters—a crucial voting bloc in the closest election to date. Kennedy's promise to "get the nation moving again" amidst an economic slowdown resonated with voters who were anxious about the economy. While not as urgent as it is in the twenty-first century, concerns about the environment and the preservation of natural resources were starting to gain importance among voters.

Internationally, the Cold War was the dominant issue. The Soviets successfully launched the first satellite, Sputnik, in 1957, and the subsequent U-2 spy plane incident of 1960 spurred major concerns over the two global powers potentially engaging in nuclear war. The Castro regime in Cuba exacerbated these concerns, as he closely aligned the island nation ninety miles off the coast of the US with the Soviet Union.

When Kennedy became president, the country was in the midst of an economic recession. He proposed tax cuts and increased federal spending to invigorate the sluggish economy, which did help, but he faced resistance from Congress on some of his economic proposals. With Southern Democrats gaining influence, Kennedy struggled to advance civil rights, a key issue on which he had campaigned.

In foreign affairs, the Bay of Pigs, a CIA-backed operation to overthrow Fidel Castro's regime, ended in disaster, with many Cuban exiles killed or captured. His decision not to provide US air support made him appear weak and contributed to a loss of confidence in his leadership. This was perhaps JFK's biggest blunder.

Following the Bay of Pigs, tensions escalated between the Soviets, Cuba, and the United States. The US identified Soviet missiles in Cuba, which brought the world to the brink of nuclear war. JFK handled the Cuban Missile Crisis with a mix of military firmness and diplomacy. A naval blockade of Cuba ultimately resulted in a peaceful resolution, but it highlighted the precarious nature of US-Soviet relations during the Cold War.

In 1961, Soviet leader Nikita Khrushchev ordered the construction of the Berlin Wall, a significant symbol of the Cold War, to prevent East Berlin citizens from escaping into West Berlin and, ultimately, into West Germany. Kennedy's commitment to defending West Berlin was crucial in maintaining US credibility in Europe.

DECISION

The decision not to immediately attack Cuba or the Soviet Union at the onset of the Cuban Missile Crisis was the most critical decision John F. Kennedy made as president.

IMPACT

JFK faced immense pressure to respond militarily to the missiles discovered by surveillance planes flying over Cuba. Instead of opting for an immediate attack, he chose a naval blockade and pursued back-channel diplomacy to resolve the crisis. This decision not only averted a nuclear war but also showcased JFK's ability to manage high-stakes international crises. His leadership during this period is often credited with improving US-Soviet relations in the long term, solidifying his reputation as a decisive leader, and averting a possible nuclear disaster. Thus, the Cuban Missile Crisis had a lasting impact on international relations, military strategy, and domestic policy.

Some of these include establishing the Washington-Moscow Hotline, the 1963 Partial Nuclear Test Ban Treaty, and the Treaty on the Non-Proliferation of Nuclear Weapons, which led to détente — a period of relaxed tensions with the Soviet Union.

The near-use of nuclear weaponry caused a massive shift in US military ideology, whereby it was realized that diplomacy had to be the primary course of action and was essential to preventing a nuclear war.

The Cuban Missile Crisis quickly and dramatically raised public awareness of the potential for nuclear disaster. JFK's adept handling of the crisis strengthened his image as a strong leader, which enhanced his public support and political capital.

Unfortunately, on November 22, 1963, a man named Lee Harvey Oswald hid in the Texas School Book Depository in Dallas, Texas. As Kennedy's motorcade passed, he fired shots with a rifle, hitting Kennedy in the neck and head. Kennedy was rushed to the hospital, where he died a half hour after the shooting.

LYNDON B. JOHNSON

THIRTY-SIXTH PRESIDENT
DEMOCRATIC PARTY
TERM: 1963–1969
YEAR OF THE DECISION: 1964

CIRCUMSTANCE

The shocking and violent death of John F. Kennedy swiftly brought Lyndon Baines Johnson (LBJ) to the presidency. He was sworn in on Air Force One, the US president's airplane, with Kennedy's widow, Jackie, still in her bloodstained outfit at his side. The country was stunned and horrified.

Raised in central Texas, Johnson developed compassion for those struggling with poverty while teaching students of Mexican descent. Compassion for the underserved was a recurring theme throughout his presidency.

Following his brief tenure as a teacher, LBJ decided to enter politics and developed a network of Congressmen, newspapermen, lobbyists, and friends, which included aides to President Franklin D. Roosevelt. He was a Roosevelt Democrat. Johnson was elected to the House of Representatives and served there for twelve years before being elected to the Senate for another twelve years. He was politically adept, becoming the youngest Senate minority leader and, upon the Democrats' victory in the Senate, majority leader. His experience and origins in a Southern state were essential to his being tapped as JFK's running mate.

He held certain responsibilities as vice president, but he was never part of Kennedy's inner circle of advisors. LBJ took charge of the space program, whose mission was to send a man to the moon and return him safely to earth; oversaw negotiations on the Partial Nuclear Test Ban Treaty; and worked to push through equal opportunity legislation for minorities. He strongly supported Kennedy's decision to send American military advisors to South Vietnam to help fend off Communism.

As president, LBJ ushered several of Kennedy's agenda items through Congress as well as several social equality programs, which he labeled the "Great Society." LBJ signed the Civil Rights Act of 1964, the first effective civil rights law since Reconstruction. This was followed by the Voting Rights Act of 1965, which gave further protections to minority voters. Medicare and Medicaid legislation were both passed under Johnson.

Vietnam was an especially thorny issue for LBJ. It consumed his presidency, as he micromanaged the escalating war in painstaking detail. The media criticized his administration's handling of the war. Anti-war protests sprang up on college campuses and in cities around the country. By 1968, more than 500,000 US troops were in Vietnam, with the death and destruction broadcast nightly on the evening news. This marked the first time the US public saw the horrors of war on television. In

January 1968, the North Vietnamese started a major military initiative called the Tet Offensive, which caused Johnson to rethink his presidency and reelection.

On March 31, 1968, Johnson stunned the country by going on national television to announce that he would not seek reelection, as he wanted to devote the rest of his term to managing his presidential responsibilities, especially the Vietnam War. As a "lame duck president," Johnson got one more major legislative victory with the passage of the Fair Housing Act of 1968, which prohibited discrimination in the sale, rental, and financing of housing based on race, religion, national origin, and sex.

DECISION

At the end of 1964, Johnson supported a strategy of "graduated response" that would gradually increase military intensity in Vietnam. This was his most crucial decision as president, because it led to hundreds of thousands of troops being sent to Vietnam. This had both short- and long-term effects on a deeply divided nation.

Johnson's surprise decision not to seek the Democratic nomination for president in 1968 changed history as well. Johnson stated that he needed to focus on his presidential duties and the Vietnam War, rather than partisan politics.

IMPACT

Even though Johnson's domestic agenda changed American society through many civil rights legislative victories, his decision to escalate the Vietnam War had a profound effect on the country and LBJ personally.

Reports of North Vietnamese attacks on US ships in

the Gulf of Tonkin in 1964 caused LBJ to ask Congress for broad military powers in Vietnam. This led to a large buildup of American troops in the conflict and a prolonged and controversial war that resulted in over 50,000 US casualties and great political strife within the United States. The war seemed to have changed the culture of American society.

RICHARD NIXON

THIRTY-SEVENTH PRESIDENT
REPUBLICAN PARTY
TERM: 1969–1974
YEAR OF THE DECISION: 1974

CIRCUMSTANCE

The Vietnam War was raging. The nation was in a state of shock following the 1968 assassinations of Civil Rights Movement leader Martin Luther King, Jr., and presidential candidate Robert F. Kennedy. There was civil unrest and protests over the Vietnam War, particularly among college-age young adults. The Cold War and efforts to halt the spread of Communism were ongoing, while poverty and unemployment were high in minority communities. A philosophical and political divide was widening between the establishment and the youth, who wanted more say over their future.

Lyndon Johnson decided not to run for reelection, and the Democrats nominated Vice President Hubert Humphrey as their candidate. George Wallace, a Southern conservative, ran as an independent. Republicans nominated Richard M. Nixon, a former Congressman,

Senator, and vice president under popular Eisenhower. These positions, plus his experience running against JFK in 1960, brought the Republican Party together under Nixon.

He ran an effective campaign with Maryland Governor Spiro Agnew as his running mate. They highlighted the nation's high crime rate and the Democrats perceived surrender of nuclear superiority to the Soviets. Nixon promised a "peace with honor" conclusion to the war in Vietnam.

During his presidency, Nixon dealt with the Vietnam War. Leading the effort was his highly visible and brilliant national security advisor and Secretary of State, Henry Kissinger. Through a series of negotiations led by Kissinger, all parties involved in the war agreed to the Paris Peace Accords, which called for the withdrawal of all US forces from Vietnam. This left the South Vietnamese to fight for themselves; they lost with the fall of Saigon in 1975. The last US personnel were evacuated from Saigon on April 30, 1975. Dramatic televised shots showed the desperation of people trying to board helicopters as they left the country.

Facing a Democratic Congress, much of Nixon's domestic agenda failed. While not initially showing much interest in environmental concerns, Nixon sensed a political opportunity after the millions of demonstrations across the country on 1970s Earth Day. The Clean Air Act of 1970 was approved, and two new agencies, the Department of Natural Resources and the Environmental Protection Agency, were created.

Nixon wanted to consolidate the power of the presidency and took the attitude that the executive branch was exempt from many of the checks and balances imposed by the Constitution. This position did not earn him favors or popularity and would adversely impact him during the Watergate scandal.

The Nixon presidency excelled in foreign policy. Aided by Kissinger, Nixon was able to lower the political temperature with China and the Soviet Union. He believed the Cold War balance of power could be altered in favor of the West, and he sent secret messages to Chinese officials to initiate a dialogue.

In 1970, trade restrictions against China were reduced, and in 1971, Chinese officials invited the American table tennis team to China for a demonstration/competition, later dubbed "Ping-Pong Diplomacy." In 1972, President Nixon and his wife, Pat, traveled to China for a summit meeting with direct talks with Mao Zedong, the leader of China. The visit and the resulting improved Chinese-American relations also pressured the Soviet Union to establish better relations with the United States as well.

Then came Watergate. The Watergate scandal involved the Nixon administration's attempts to cover up its involvement in the 1972 break-in at the Democratic National Committee headquarters at the Watergate Office Building in Washington, DC. Investigations uncovered a relationship between the burglars and the Nixon administration. It also unveiled how the Nixon administration had abused its authority, including illegal wiretapping, using government agencies to harass political opponents, and attempting to use the CIA to impede the FBI's investigation.

Members of his administration used "slush money"

from the Committee to Re-Elect the President to conduct various unethical activities, including covering up the break-in at Watergate and financing "dirty tricks" against political opponents. Ultimately, some of Nixon's closest advisors and government officials, including his attorney general, John Mitchell, were imprisoned for their involvement. Carl Bernstein and Bob Woodward, investigative journalists with the Washington Post, "followed the money" and received tips from an FBI insider using the pseudonym "Deep Throat," all of which ultimately led directly to Nixon. As evidence of the cover-up mounted, including the revelation of secret White House tapes, there was significant public outrage, and Nixon faced likely impeachment. Congressional hearings, televised live, brought the events into the homes of millions of Americans.

Rather than being impeached and removed from office, Nixon resigned the presidency on August 8, 1974, and left office the next day.

DECISION

Participating in the events surrounding the Watergate scandal and its subsequent cover-up, which led to his being the first president to resign from office, was Nixon's most important decision as president.

IMPACT

Nixon's resignation was the first and only time in US history that a president resigned from office, and was thus an unprecedented, historical event. It greatly affected American history in a number of ways.

After the trauma of the Vietnam War, followed by

the Watergate scandal, America was relieved that the country could finally move forward with a new leader. Gerald Ford became president when the Twenty-Fifth Amendment was used for the first time to fill a presidential vacancy.

During Watergate, many Americans became disillusioned with the government, especially after seeing numerous Nixon appointees being prosecuted for criminal activity. The actions of these high-ranking government officials damaged public trust, which led to legislation providing new oversight of the executive branch. Some of the new legislation included the Foreign Intelligence Surveillance Act of 1978, which regulates government surveillance activities. Law schools began to add and require courses on professional ethics for attorneys. The American Bar Association rewrote its code of professional responsibility.

The Watergate scandal boosted the reputation of journalists and made celebrities of reporters like Carl Bernstein and Bob Woodward, who gained fame for their investigative work. Their fame was further heightened by the book All the President's Men, which was adapted into a movie starring Robert Redford and Dustin Hoffman.

This scandal also had an impact on the English language. Henceforth, scandals were commonly named by adding the suffix "-gate" to a word.

The role of the Supreme Court in limiting executive power was demonstrated by its unanimous decision ordering President Nixon to release the White House tapes related to the Watergate scandal. That decision directly led to Nixon's resignation, as he lost support in Congress when the transcripts of the recordings were released.

Gerald Ford already had a reputation for integrity, and his approval ratings rose as the country witnessed a peaceful transfer of power to a well-respected man.

GERALD FORD

THIRTY-EIGHTH PRESIDENT
REPUBLICAN PARTY
TERM: 1974–1977
YEAR OF THE DECISION: 1974

CIRCUMSTANCE

Richard Nixon's resignation was unprecedented. His vice president, Gerald R. Ford, had been chosen under the terms of the Twenty-Fifth Amendment, as he had not been directly elected to the office of vice president. Ford was widely respected for his honesty, integrity, and transparency, which made him popular in Congress, where he had served for twenty-five years. Even so, Ford was largely unknown to the general public when he assumed the highest office in the land.

Domestically, in addition to the aftermath of the tumultuous Watergate scandal, inflation was on the rise, and the economy was sinking. Ford attempted to curb inflation, but when that effort failed and the country fell into a recession, he pivoted to alternative means to get the economy moving again.

Toward the end of 1973, a new war erupted in the Middle East between Israel and a coalition of Arab countries led by Egypt and Syria. Preventing yet another war in the Middle East was Ford's priority. He authorized aid to both Israel and Egypt, which helped persuade the two countries to accept an interim truce agreement.

Détente with the Soviet Union was ongoing, and Ford had a summit with Soviet leader Leonid I. Brezhnev to set new limits on nuclear weapons. He was also the first US president to visit Japan.

A month after taking office, Ford made a decision that had a profoundly adverse impact on his reputation for integrity. He granted Richard Nixon a presidential pardon, which absolved Nixon of criminal liability in the Watergate scandal and left the country wondering if a deal had been struck beforehand. Many questioned whether Ford was truly pursuing the country's best interests by putting Nixon's Watergate liabilities in the rearview mirror.

DECISION

In one of the most controversial decisions a United States president has ever made, Ford pardoned Richard Nixon for criminal liability related to the Watergate break-in and cover-up.

IMPACT

The public deeply condemned the pardon of Richard Nixon for many reasons. Among them was the concern that a backroom deal had been struck to make Ford president. Ford testified before Congress that no agreement had been made. Even so, many believed that no one is above the law, including a sitting US president.

The pardon of Nixon seemed to contradict this axiom.

Ford was under the impression that acceptance of a pardon was an admission of guilt, a conclusion supported by a prior Supreme Court ruling. Bringing closure to the Watergate scandal and allowing the country to move forward was Ford's justification for the pardon.

Politically, Ford's pardon of Nixon backfired. This decision severely tarnished his reputation and cast a shadow over his administration for the remainder of his term. His approval ratings tanked. When Ford ran for reelection, he faced considerable flak for his decision from all the Republican primary candidates, including future President Ronald Reagan. Nonetheless, Ford did become the Republican nominee, but he was defeated by Jimmy Carter.

JIMMY CARTER

THIRTY-NINTH PRESIDENT
DEMOCRATIC PARTY
TERM: 1977–1981
YEAR OF THE DECISION: 1979

CIRCUMSTANCE

James ("Jimmy") Earl Carter was born and raised on a peanut farm in the small town of Plains, Georgia, where talk of politics and practicing the Baptist religion were bastions of life. Carter graduated from the US Naval Academy and took graduate courses in reactor technology and nuclear physics while serving in the Navy for seven years.

Upon his discharge, he entered local politics and was eventually elected governor of Georgia. As a young governor, he supported programs in ecology, government efficiency, and civil rights. In 1974, he started a two-year-long bid for the presidency with Midwestern Senator Walter Mondale as his running mate. With a nation still divided over Ford's handling of Watergate and being critical of Ford's economic policies, Carter cruised to victory. He entered office with high approval ratings, as Americans felt they were "turning the corner" and had finally left Watergate and a poor economy behind.

Foreign policy and its impact on the US economy dominated Carter's administration. The country was still feeling the lingering effects of a 1973 oil embargo by the Arab-dominated Organization of Petroleum Exporting Countries (OPEC), caused by US support of Israel during the 1973 Yom Kippur War. As a result, Carter focused his domestic agenda on energy. He succeeded in slightly reducing foreign oil consumption and initiated the development of the US Strategic Energy Reserve, which stores huge quantities of emergency oil and natural gas.

President Carter mediated the 1978 Camp David Accords between Israel and Egypt. These meetings resulted in a historic peace treaty, whereby Israel withdrew from the Sinai Peninsula, and Egypt and Israel recognized each other's governments.

Under Carter, full diplomatic relations with the People's Republic of China were established, and the second round of the Strategic Arms Limitation Talks (SALT II) was concluded.

Carter was mired in Middle Eastern politics throughout his presidency, particularly with the Iranian Revolution of 1979, which saw the overthrow of the US-supported shah of Iran. This conflict and its aftermath gave rise to enormous strife for Carter and the country. Iranian revolutionaries stormed the US embassy in Tehran. They seized sixty-six members of the embassy staff and held fifty-two of them for fourteen months, releasing the others on medical or humanitarian grounds. This was known as the Iranian Hostage Crisis, and it dominated the news during this period.

The Iranian Hostage Crisis had severe diplomatic repercussions. Carter severed diplomatic relations with Iran and imposed economic sanctions, including the freezing of Iranian assets. The US initiated an international diplomatic campaign against Iran, securing United Nations Security Council resolutions condemning the hostage-taking. Iran retaliated by preventing the US from accessing its oil, which caused a severe gasoline shortage and long lines at gas stations.

A desperate Carter authorized Operation Eagle Claw, which was a failed rescue attempt. The US military rescue operation ended tragically, and eight American servicemen perished when a helicopter crashed in the Iranian desert.

The Iranian Hostage Crisis ingrained suspicion, distrust, and hostility toward Iran, which continues in the US even now. The crisis undermined confidence in President Carter and made him appear weak.

Although Carter sought a second term as president, he was severely challenged in the Democratic primaries by US Senator Edward Kennedy, the popular younger brother of JFK and RFK. Kennedy refused to concede the nomination until the second day of the Democratic National Convention. Carter won the primaries but ultimately lost the election to former California Governor Ronald Reagan.

DECISION

Carter made a series of poor decisions during the Iranian Hostage Crisis, all of which led to it escalating.

IMPACT

When the Iranian Revolution began, the Shah escaped first to Egypt and then to Morocco, where he was welcomed as a guest. The Iranian revolutionaries demanded the extradition of the exiled Shah, but Carter struggled to formulate a coherent response, leading to a perception of indecisiveness.

Following a diagnosis of cancer, the Shah requested entrance to the US for medical treatment. Carter's approval of this request was a pivotal decision that escalated the crisis. State Department officials had warned him that there would likely be repercussions from Iran for this decision. The shah's admission intensified anti-American sentiments in Iran and led directly to the storming of the US embassy in Tehran, where sixty-six Americans were taken hostage.

Carter set a policy of restraint and diplomacy, prioritizing the hostages' safety over aggressive military action. This approach aimed to preserve American honor, but it was criticized as ineffective and was likely seen as weakness by Iran and other countries.

Through the news media, the American public was regularly reminded of the hostage situation, which became a symbol of national humiliation. This ongoing news coverage contributed to a sense of despair and frustration among the population.

The hostage crisis contributed to and coincided with economic problems, including high inflation and energy shortages. The politically charged environment highlighted Carter's inability to resolve the crisis and was seen as a failure of leadership. Carter's Republican challenger, Ronald Reagan, made the Iranian Hostage

Crisis a political focal point and capitalized on Carter's struggle to resolve the matter.

The hostages were released on the day of Ronald Reagan's inauguration, leading to speculation that the Iranian government had delayed their release to undermine Carter's reelection bid.

RONALD REAGAN

THIRTY-NINTH PRESIDENT
REPUBLICAN PARTY
TERM: 1981–1989
YEAR OF THE DECISION: 1986

CIRCUMSTANCE

Ronald Wilson Reagan had a thirty-year career as an actor, in which he appeared in over fifty movies. He served as president of the Screen Actors Guild (SAG), which gave him a taste of politics. Although he started with a liberal democratic philosophy, he was staunchly anti-Communist. Reagan's transition from his role at SAG to a career in governmental politics was gradual, but he eventually became a two-term governor of California. Over time, his political bent became more conservative.

Reagan sought the Republican nomination for president in 1968 and 1976 but lost both times. However, 1980 was his year. The growth of the conservative base and high dissatisfaction with Jimmy Carter allowed him to win the election and become the fortieth US president.

Reagan ran on a platform of "peace through strength,"

which gave him leeway to criticize the failed policies of his predecessor, set a new approach to limited federal government, and also build military and diplomatic strength. He chose the skilled former Texas Congressman and United Nations Ambassador George H.W. Bush as his running mate. In an election landslide, Reagan won 489 electoral votes to President Jimmy Carter's 49. The election results showed a complete rejection of Carter's presidency, especially his handling of the Iranian Hostage Crisis, whose captives were released the day of Reagan's inauguration.

Only sixty-nine days into Reagan's presidency, a would-be assassin shot and severely wounded the president. He quickly recovered and returned to work. His wit, attitude, and demeanor to the whole affair ingratiated him with the American public.

Reagan passed legislation to promote economic growth, curb inflation, increase employment, and build up the military. In the spirit of making government smaller, he cut taxes and reduced overall government spending. He refused to change his agenda and maintained a large budget for the military, despite it resulting in a substantial and concerning fiscal deficit.

Always a complex problem, the Middle East was especially difficult for Reagan. In 1982, he sent 800 US Marines to Lebanon as part of an international peacekeeping force. One year later, suicide bombers attacked the Marine barracks in Beirut, killing 241 Americans.

In another mission, Reagan ordered US forces to invade the Caribbean island of Grenada after Marxist rebels overthrew the government. The island was liberated.

During his second term, Reagan worked to improve

relations with the Soviet Union. In summits with Soviet leader Mikhail Gorbachev, they agreed to a treaty that eliminated intermediate-range nuclear missiles. In 1987, he stood in front of the Berlin Wall in West Berlin and challenged Gorbachev to "tear down this wall." Two years later, Soviet domination of East Germany ended when Gorbachev allowed the Berlin Wall to be dismantled.

By sending American bombers to Libya based on evidence that it was involved in an attack on American soldiers in a West Berlin nightclub, he demonstrated that his declaration of war on terrorism was no joke.

Reagan inherited a terrible economy from Carter. Interest rates were incredibly high, with the prime rate over 20 percent; inflation was rampant; unemployment was over 7 percent; productivity was declining; and government spending was growing rapidly. Reagan instituted a series of economic reforms called "Reaganomics." These included tax cuts, especially for high earners, reduced government spending, deregulation, the elimination of price controls, and increased military spending. His "trickle-down" economic theory was a novel concept, whereby government assistance to the wealthy and businesses would result in improvements to the financial status of all levels of society. Thus, the money would "flow downward" to the masses.

Reagan's presidency was not without scandal, as the Iran-Contra affair tarnished his second term. This was an illegal and convoluted "arms-for-hostages" deal with Iran that then funneled money toward anti-Communist insurgencies in Central America.

Reagan utilized his theatrical skills, along with a sense

of humor, to conduct a presidency with a serious sense of purpose while also endearing himself to the American people. He was known as the "Great Communicator" due to his ability to simplify complex issues in a way that the general public could understand. Ronald Reagan became a conservative icon and the standard to which other politicians were held.

DECISION

Reagan's decision to change the world order by ending the Cold War was the most consequential of his presidency. The pivotal meeting with Soviet General Secretary Mikhail Gorbachev at the Reykjavik Summit in 1986 marked a turning point in the general decline of the Soviet Union.

IMPACT

Reagan advocated for a balance of strength and diplomacy in negotiating with the Soviets. He had the unusual opportunity to be paired with a reformist Soviet leader, Gorbachev, who had recently come to power.

Reagan's buildup of the US military sent a strong signal to the Soviets and the world that the United States was serious about its defense and that of NATO and its other allies. His "peace through strength" strategy gave him a position of power in the negotiations.

His dramatic proposal of the Strategic Defense Initiative (SDI), also known as "Star Wars," put pressure on the Soviet Union to compete technologically and economically, placing great strain on its economy.

His empathy and goodwill toward Gorbachev's reform efforts helped reassure Soviet leadership that their security would not be endangered as they reshaped their political and economic systems.

However, it was Reagan's belief in capitalism and his aggressive buildup of the military that ultimately led to the economic collapse and the dismantling of the Soviet Union. This resulted in former Soviet states becoming free democratic societies.

GEORGE H.W. BUSH

FORTY-FIRST PRESIDENT
REPUBLICAN PARTY
TERM: 1989–1993
YEAR OF THE DECISION: 1990

CIRCUMSTANCE

Following his successor's successful presidency, George H.W. Bush (aka, Bush 41)—a businessman, Congressman, former head of the CIA, Ambassador to the United Nations, and vice president under Reagan—was elected president. As a highly experienced government servant and politician, Bush 41 had an excellent understanding of domestic and foreign policy. His platform included no new taxes, as he famously pledged during his speech accepting the Republican nomination: "Read my lips: no new taxes."

His goal was to make the United States a "kinder and gentler nation." As such, in his inaugural address, he introduced the concept of a "thousand points of light" to encourage community service and volunteerism.

George H. W. Bush had the distinction of being the youngest pilot in the US Navy when he received his wings. He flew fifty-eight combat missions in World War II, and on one mission, he was shot down over the Pacific by Japanese anti-aircraft fire. He was rescued from the water by a U.S submarine.

The world was changing as George H.W. Bush became president. The Soviet Union was collapsing, and the Berlin Wall fell not long after he entered office.

Bush sent American troops to Panama to overthrow the corrupt regime of General Manuel Noriega, who threatened the security of the Panama Canal and the Americans living in the country. In a dramatic military operation, Noriega was captured and brought to the United States for trial, where he was convicted of drug trafficking.

Iraqi President Saddam Hussein invaded oil-rich Kuwait in 1990 and threatened to go into Saudi Arabia as well. Bush 41 rallied the United Nations, the US people, and Congress, sending 425,000 American troops to the Middle East. An additional 118,000 soldiers from allied nations participated in the Gulf War. After weeks of air and missile bombardment, a one-hundred-hour land battle ensued, dubbed Operation Desert Storm, which successfully ejected Iraqi forces from Kuwait. However, Hussein remained in power.

Despite the victory in Kuwait, the US economy was slowing down, and the country was facing a significant budget deficit. Regretting his famous "Read my lips" line, Bush 41 agreed to a budget compromise that included tax increases. Many of his constituents saw this as a betrayal, and Bush 41 was not reelected.

DECISION

The most critical decision that George H.W. Bush made as president was to utilize the US military to eject Iraqi forces from the US ally Kuwait.

IMPACT

Bush 41's decision to defend Kuwait and invade Iraq in the 1990–1991 Gulf War had several significant impacts.

First, it achieved its primary objective of expelling Iraqi forces from Kuwait, restoring the oil-producing country's sovereignty and independence. Second, it demonstrated that diplomatic efforts could bring a coalition of nations together to rectify an injustice committed by an aggressor nation. This is considered one of his most significant foreign policy achievements. Third, by preventing Iraq from controlling Kuwait's oil reserves, Bush 41 protected about 20 percent of the world's oil supply from falling under Iraqi control.

In the scope of wars, it was short, with the ground campaign lasting only about one hundred hours. The quick victory boosted Bush 41's approval ratings. While Hussein remained in power, the war greatly weakened Iraq's military capabilities. The intervention restored the Middle Eastern balance of power to its pre-intervention status quo and reassured US Middle Eastern allies, particularly Saudi Arabia.

Even though he achieved his goal of removing Iraqi forces from Kuwait, Bush 41 faced heavy criticism for not removing Saddam Hussein from power or annihilating Iraq's military. The ongoing stationing of US forces in Saudi Arabia after the war became a source of tension in the region. It was later cited by al-Qaeda as a motivation for the 9/11 attacks.

The war led to fluctuations in oil prices, resulting in economic instability, which contributed to his reelection defeat.

BILL CLINTON

FORTY-SECOND PRESIDENT
DEMOCRATIC PARTY
TERM: 1993–2001
YEAR OF THE DECISION: 1993

CIRCUMSTANCE

An excellent student and proficient saxophone player, William Jefferson Clinton, born in Hope, Arkansas, once considered a career as a professional musician. He was, however, inspired by a White House Rose Garden meeting with John F. Kennedy and decided that politics would be his life's work. A Rhodes Scholarship at Oxford University and a law degree from Yale gave Bill Clinton the credentials he needed to enter politics at a young age. He married Hillary Rodham, a fellow Yale Law School graduate.

Being elected attorney general of Arkansas in 1976 positioned him to win the governorship in 1978. He lost his bid for a second term as governor but regained the office four years later. Then, he decided to make a bid for the presidency.

Clinton's platform aimed to boost the sluggish economy by improving the financial situation of the middle class. He also advocated for job growth, welfare reform, and healthcare reform. During his campaign, a defining moment arose when James Carville, one of Clinton's advisors, famously told the candidate, "It's the economy, stupid," to focus him on the singular key issue of importance to the American public.

The 1992 presidential race included Bush 41 and the charismatic billionaire independent candidate, Ross Perot. Perot's positions on balancing the federal budget, economic nationalism, and implementing "electronic town halls" for direct democracy induced 20 percent of the population to vote for him, enough to draw a substantial number of votes away from Bush 41.

Clinton selected another Southerner, the forty-four-year-old Tennessee Senator Albert Gore, Jr., as his running mate, and the two positioned themselves as a new generation of political leaders. With their victory, the executive branch and Congress were held by the same party for the first time in twelve years. This political advantage was brief, though, as Republicans won both houses of Congress in 1994.

Making a major political mistake, Clinton appointed his wife the head of the task force for healthcare reform in 1993. The public resented that Clinton had placed his wife, a virtual unknown and unelected person, in such an important position. Hillary Clinton developed a plan that proposed universal health coverage through a mandate requiring employers to provide health insurance to their employees—a policy frequently referred to as "Hillarycare." Businesses did not want to take on another financial burden, and the legislation failed.

The first Democratic president to win a second term since Franklin D. Roosevelt, Clinton's economic policies resulted in the lowest unemployment and lowest inflation in thirty years, the highest home ownership rate ever, declining crime rates, and lower welfare rolls. Economically, he achieved a budget surplus. Clinton also called for improvements in civil rights.

In 1995, Clinton became involved in a sexual relationship with a twenty-two-year-old intern named Monica Lewinsky. Their two-year relationship was revealed in 1998. Kenneth Starr was appointed as an independent counsel to investigate the relationship and discovered that Lewinsky had confided in Linda Tripp, a civil servant holdover from the Bush 41 administration. Tripp secretly recorded their conversations and later provided these tapes to Starr.

Clinton denied the allegations, stating, "I did not have sexual relations with that woman, Ms. Lewinsky." In a televised address in August 1998, Clinton did admit to having an "inappropriate" relationship with Lewinsky. Previously, Clinton had been deposed about the matter and gave false or misleading answers. The deposition, along with Starr's investigation, led to the House of Representatives impeaching him on charges of perjury and obstruction of justice. The Senate trial began in January 1999, and Clinton was acquitted, as the votes did not reach the two-thirds majority needed to convict him.

DECISION

Both before and after the 1992 election, Clinton's recognition that "It's the economy, stupid" was his most important decision as president.

IMPACT

Clinton's focus on the economic issues of the day enabled him to achieve excellent fiscal results. He reduced the federal deficit, created a surplus, and entered the North American Free Trade Agreement (NAFTA), which opened foreign markets. He also invested in the middle class, helping to create the conditions for an extended period of economic growth. He also deregulated the finance industry.

The Clinton economy benefited from the era's tremendous advances in technology, especially the mainstreaming of the personal computer. This essentially put a large mainframe computer of the past on the desks of regular employees, generating dramatic increases in worker productivity. Clinton's economic reforms created more than twenty-two million jobs and led to the longest peacetime economic expansion in American history, lasting almost ten years.

GEORGE W. BUSH

FORTY-THIRD PRESIDENT
REPUBLICAN PARTY
TERM: 2001–2009
YEAR OF THE DECISION: 2001

CIRCUMSTANCE

After the 1992 election of Bill Clinton, President George H.W. Bush's son, George W. Bush (also known as Bush 43), decided to run for governor of Texas as a Republican. With his victory, he became the first governor to be the son of a US president, and he was so popular that he was elected to consecutive four-year terms as governor—a first for Texas.

After the unprecedented peace and prosperity of the Clinton presidency, it was no surprise that Vice President Al Gore would run for president in 2000. Bush 43 also entered the presidential election and ran on the philosophy of "compassionate conservatism," which combined ideals of limited government and personal responsibility with concern for the underprivileged. His moderate approach and strong image made him competitive with Gore.

Among the most contested presidential elections in history, George W. Bush was awarded the presidency by the Supreme Court following a month-long post-election legal battle regarding the validity of ballots. After the Supreme Court ruling, Gore decided to gracefully decline to pursue additional legal challenges.

On September 11, 2001, al-Qaeda terrorists hijacked four US commercial airliners, three of which hit their targets at the World Trade Center buildings in New York and the Pentagon in Washington, DC. A fourth hijacked plane was brought down into a field in Pennsylvania by its rebelling passengers. Almost three thousand innocent Americans were killed in that day's attacks. For the first time in history, NATO implemented Article 5 of its treaty, which states that an armed attack against one NATO member nation is considered an attack against all members and obligates them to respond collectively. Thus, the US gained NATO and generally worldwide support in its efforts to counter the threat.

In this moment, Bush 43 was transformed from a peacetime president to a wartime president.

Bush 43 created the new Cabinet-level Department of Homeland Security, which integrated the intelligence agencies and other functions. He sent American forces into Afghanistan to break up the Taliban, a political/religious movement that gave shelter to al-Qaeda's leader, Osama bin Laden. The Taliban trained, financed, and exported terrorists, including those who were responsible for the attacks on September 11. The Taliban was successfully disrupted, but bin Laden escaped.

Bush 43's most controversial decision was part of his Global War on Terror. Acting on intelligence suggesting that Iraq had biological and/or nuclear weapons, he ordered an invasion of Iraq. Saddam Hussein, the president of Iraq, was captured, tried, and hanged, but the disruption of Iraq and the killing of American military forces by insurgents became a serious challenge. Bush 43 declared an end to primary combat operations in Iraq in May 2003, and with a power vacuum in place, Iraq soon fell into a sectarian civil war.

As a corollary to the Global War on Terror, Bush 43 proclaimed that the United States would preemptively use military force to prevent threats to its national security by terrorists or "rogue states," especially any that possessed weapons of mass destruction or harbored suspected terrorists.

Bush 43 ran successfully for reelection, defeating John Kerry, an esteemed Democratic Senator. During his second term, Bush 43 pursued immigration reform, which received criticism from many conservatives, and relaxed environmental regulations, prompting criticism from liberals. The Bush administration's poor response to Hurricane Katrina, which destroyed much of New Orleans and the surrounding areas, demonstrably hurt Bush 43's reputation.

Fighting two foreign wars—Iraq and Afghanistan—depleted the budget surplus Clinton had left and transformed it into a multi-trillion-dollar debt. In 2008, the country was hit with a severe credit crisis that sent the stock market into rapid decline, resulting in massive layoffs, particularly in the financial sector. Bush 43 hurried to develop and pass the controversial $700 billion Emergency Economic Stabilization Act to bail out the housing and banking industries.

DECISION

The most important decision that George W. Bush made as president was his response to the September 11, 2001, terrorist attacks and the resultant launch of the Global War on Terror. This decision had far-reaching consequences that shaped much of his presidency and American foreign policy for years to come.

IMPACT

The Global War on Terror became the focus of Bush 43's presidency, with the wars in Afghanistan and Iraq becoming the longest conflicts in US history. The US formed a coalition of nations to fight terrorism, and NATO implemented Article 5 of its treaty for the first time. America froze the assets of terrorist groups and individuals. A total of 196 countries officially supported these efforts, and 142 countries also took steps to freeze terrorist assets.

The Iraq War was highly controversial, especially when no weapons of mass destruction were found. This tarnished Bush 43's legacy.

Bush 43 put the world on notice that any nation harboring terrorists or supporting terrorism would be regarded as hostile.

The Department of Homeland Security was created to integrate the US intelligence agencies into a singular department. The Patriot Act and other national security measures sparked debates about civil liberties. These led to effective counterterrorism measures that impacted diplomatic, financial, and military actions globally.

The financial impact of the Global War on Terror was substantial. A Congressional Budget Office report estimated that the US wars in Iraq and Afghanistan cost taxpayers a total of $2.4 trillion, with about $1.9 trillion being spent on Iraq.

By the 2008 election, the economy was in the midst of the Great Recession, marked by a severe financial crisis, a collapse in housing prices, and a significant downturn in economic activity. It brought widespread unemployment and a sharp decline in GDP. This resulted in the failures of major financial institutions, a severe credit crunch, and a drop in consumer and business confidence. The 2008 bankruptcy of Lehman Brothers, a brokerage house, shook the financial world and exacerbated the global financial crisis.

BARACK OBAMA

FORTY-FOURTH PRESIDENT
DEMOCRATIC PARTY
TERM: 2009–2017
YEAR OF THE DECISION: 2009

CIRCUMSTANCE

Barack Obama was the first African American to be elected President of the United States. From the fifth grade on, he was raised in Honolulu by his maternal grandparents. Obama was smart and ambitious. He attended Columbia University, where he studied political science and international relations. After working as a community advocate in Chicago, he attended Harvard Law School, where he garnered national attention as the first African American president of the Harvard Law Review. After Harvard, Obama joined a small law firm in Chicago that specialized in civil rights. He also taught Constitutional law part-time at the University of Chicago Law School and helped organize voter registration drives during Clinton's 1992 presidential campaign. In 1992, Obama married Michelle Robinson, another Harvard Law graduate.

His advocacy work won him a seat in the Illinois State Senate. Then, in 2004, he ran for and won the US Senate seat that a Republican had just vacated. Obama gave the keynote speech in support of John Kerry at the 2004 Democratic National Convention, which garnered him national attention. In 2007, he announced his candidacy for president and became embroiled in a tight primary battle with then-US Senator Hillary Clinton from New York. In 2008, Obama secured the Democratic Party's nomination, and in November of that year, he defeated Senator John McCain of Arizona and was elected president.

The domestic and foreign situations were complex as Obama entered office. The economy was in disarray, and to revive it, Obama proposed unprecedented federal intervention. Changing the way foreign nations viewed America—which had lost a great deal of credibility when weapons of mass destruction were not found in Iraq—was also one of Obama's priorities.

Obama's signature piece of domestic legislation was the Affordable Care Act, a major healthcare reform bill popularly known as "ObamaCare." In 2009, thanks to his work to reduce the threat of nuclear war and his approach to fighting climate change, Obama became the fourth president to receive the Nobel Peace Prize. In 2011, US intelligence located Osama bin Laden, the mastermind of the September 11, 2001, terror attacks on the US Obama authorized a daring raid into Pakistan, which resulted in the killing of the head of al-Qaeda.

The Middle East continued to be a key foreign policy challenge in Obama's second term. In 2014, ISIS, an extraordinarily violent and ruthless terrorist group, captured large swaths of land in Iraq and eastern Syria. Obama used military force to eliminate ISIS, but with limited effect. Obama also sought to contain the nuclear ambitions of hostile Iran with a treaty that hindered its development of these weapons. He signed the Paris Climate Accords, an international treaty signed by 195 nations with the goal of reducing greenhouse gas emissions to slow global warming and climate change. Obama also normalized relations with Cuba, reopening the US embassy in Havana in July 2015.

DECISION

Although President Obama faced many domestic and foreign challenges, his most consequential decision was his response to the Great Recession, which was ongoing when he first took office.

IMPACT

The key legislation that Obama signed to combat the Great Recession was the American Recovery and Reinvestment Act (ARRA), which was passed at a crucial moment in his presidency. This was a $787 billion stimulus package designed to prevent the country from falling into a second Great Depression. ARRA combined tax breaks with infrastructure spending, the extension of welfare benefits, and education initiatives. During the Great Recession, unemployment peaked at 10 percent but receded to 5 percent by the end of his presidency.

Obama also decided to bail out the US automobile industry. This temporarily made the government a partial owner of these large companies until they repaid the loans that had helped keep them afloat.

The Affordable Care Act and Obama's foreign policy initiatives also required bold and important decisions. Still, in the absence of the economic strategies and programs Obama enacted early in his presidency, it is highly likely that the Great Recession would have turned into a catastrophic economic depression. Therefore, his response to the economic situation proved to be pivotal and shaped much of Obama's presidency. It had far-reaching effects on the economy and the lives of everyday Americans.

DONALD TRUMP

FORTY-FIFTH PRESIDENT
REPUBLICAN PARTY
TERM: 2017–2021
YEAR OF THE DECISION: 2020

CIRCUMSTANCE

New York real-estate developer, billionaire, TV celebrity, non-lawyer, non-politician, and businessman Donald Trump developed an interest in politics. In 2015, he announced his intention to run for president. Trump fended off more than a dozen rivals to win the Republican nomination. His opponent in the general election was the odds-on favorite, former First Lady, former US Senator, and former Secretary of State under Obama, Hillary Clinton. Clinton was a divisive force, with strong supporters, but there was also a large anti-Hillary contingency, even among democrats. While Trump won a majority of Electoral College votes, he lost the popular vote. His campaign slogan was "Make America Great Again," and he positioned himself as an anti-establishment Populist candidate representing ordinary Americans.

As president, he utilized social media, especially Twitter, to communicate directly with the American public, a first for a sitting president. He successfully passed a major tax reform bill into law, reducing taxes for the wealthy while simplifying tax filing by eliminating deductions and increasing the standard deduction. Trump pressed for a reduction of federal regulations. His protectionist trade policies included tariffs on foreign products, and he renegotiated trade agreements with Mexico, Canada, China, Japan, and South Korea.

Believing it was in the country's best interests, Trump dismantled multilateral agreements to prioritize US economic interests over global initiatives. Preventing and slowing climate change was the subject of the first of many disagreements the US president had with international leaders. He also withdrew the US from the Iranian nuclear deal, which the US had agreed to under the Obama administration, and displayed his lack of support for NATO. Trump was confrontational toward China's trade practices, initiated tariffs, and renegotiated trade agreements. He replaced the North American Free Trade Agreement (NAFTA) with the United States-Mexico-Canada Agreement (USMCA). These decisions, which were all drastic departures from diplomatic norms, resulted in a complex legacy that still impacts US foreign policy.

President Trump had the unusual opportunity to nominate and have appointed three Supreme Court justices. All three were philosophically conservative. He increased the military budget and instituted aggressive border and immigration control.

President Trump took the long-discussed, but never

enacted, step of moving the US embassy in Israel from Tel Aviv to Jerusalem and, through the Abraham Accords, brokered normalization agreements between Israel and four Arab countries. He effectively neutralized the terrorist organization ISIS. President Trump attended summits with Russian President Vladimir Putin and was the first US president to meet with a North Korean leader, Kim Jong-un.

In 2019, a federal whistleblower filed a complaint that President Trump had pressured Ukrainian President Volodymyr Zelensky to investigate former Vice President Joe Biden's son Hunter for political gain. This was the basis for Trump's first impeachment: obstruction of Congress and abuse of power. In 2020, the Senate acquitted Trump on both articles.

In 2020, the COVID-19 pandemic hit the shores of the United States, and the remainder of Trump's presidency was consumed by it. Trump's response to the pandemic seemed delayed to some, and he did not encourage public health practices, such as wearing protective masks, to reduce the spread of the virus. He did, however, initiate Operation Warp Speed, in which the federal government partnered with drug companies to rapidly develop two approved vaccines. These vaccines reduced the severity of the infection but did not prevent the transmission of the disease. Trump initiated a COVID-19 stimulus package, returning tax dollars directly to US taxpayers, but this had an adverse impact on the US budget deficit. By the end of his term in office, more than 400,000 Americans had died of COVID-19.

In 2020, President Trump ran for reelection and lost to Democrat Joe Biden, but he publicly claimed that widespread voter fraud had influenced the outcome of the election. According to many news media outlets and other sources, no large-scale instances of voter fraud were found. Nonetheless, at Trump's invitation, supporters traveled to Washington, DC, for a rally on January 6, 2021. Trump and his political supporters spoke to the large crowd on the Ellipse near the White House and then encouraged attendees to walk to Congress to protest the counting of the Electoral College votes. The rally turned violent when the protestors overwhelmed law enforcement, breached the United States Capitol, and disrupted the vote count. The Capitol complex suffered millions of dollars in damage, and five people died in the incident.

In another act of protest, Trump refused to participate in the inauguration of his successor.

Afterward, the House of Representatives approved another Article of Impeachment, this one for the incitement of insurrection, making him the only president in American history to be impeached twice. For a second time, Donald Trump was acquitted by the Senate, mainly because he was out of office when the trial ended.

Subsequently, former President Trump was indicted by a special counsel appointed by the attorney general for his alleged efforts to overturn the 2020 election. These charges included conspiracy to defraud the United States, conspiracy to obstruct an official proceeding, obstruction of and attempt to obstruct an official proceeding, and conspiracy against rights. These charges arose from Trump's alleged actions to spread false claims about election fraud, void legitimate votes, disrupt the certification of the electoral vote in Congress, and "oppress, threaten, and intimidate" people in their right to vote.

In an unrelated indictment in May 2024, Donald Trump became the first former president convicted of a felony. Trump was found guilty by a Manhattan jury on thirty-four felony counts of falsifying business records.

Additionally, before his New York conviction, E. Jean Carroll, a well-known advice columnist, publicly accused Trump of rape in a 2019 article for New York Magazine. She detailed the incident that allegedly occurred in a dressing room at a New York department store. Carroll subsequently filed two lawsuits against Trump. The first focused on defamation claims related to Trump's public denials and disparaging remarks about her allegations. The second lawsuit was allowed under New York's Adult Survivors Act. It included claims of battery and defamation, allowing her to seek damages for the alleged sexual assault despite the expiration of the statute of limitations. These were both civil cases. Trump was found liable for sexual abuse and defamation, and Carroll was awarded $83.3 million in damages. This amount included $18.3 million in compensatory damages and $65 million in punitive damages.

Despite these legal troubles, Trump staged a remarkable comeback. He denied all allegations against him. Stunning many, Donald Trump won the Republican nomination in 2024 and was victorious in the general election to win back the presidency.

DECISION

The most important decision Trump made as president was to contest the 2020 election.

IMPACT

President Donald Trump refused to accept the results of the 2020 election. His ongoing and persistent claims of election fraud eroded trust in the electoral process for a large segment of the population, particularly his political base.

Donald Trump's claims about the election being stolen contributed to the violent attack on the US Capitol on January 6, 2021. His supporters, believing the election was fraudulent, stormed the Capitol in an attempt to overturn the results by encouraging the vice president, whose role in the certification process is largely procedural and ceremonial, to accept substitute electors and throw the election into the House of Representatives, as had been the case with John Quincy Adams. Vice President Mike Pence refused to do so, and the electoral certification process was temporarily halted until the violence subsided.

Trump's allegations of widespread voter fraud and "rigged" elections had a lasting effect on public trust in the US's electoral systems, particularly among Republicans. This is in spite of the fact that the president's own appointed head of election security and his own Attorney General stated that there was no evidence of voter fraud that would have impacted the outcome of the election.

These actions set a precedent in the face of allegations of election fraud, which could be followed by losing candidates, potentially destabilizing future elections by questioning the results.

Trump's post-election attempts to overturn the results put enormous pressure on state election officials, courts, and Congress, testing their resilience in upholding the will of the voters. Many Trump supporters, including influential Congressional leaders, continue to support the claims, which, according to many media sources, remain unsubstantiated.

Trump's position on the 2020 elections greatly polarized the country. This divide is still felt both on the political side, among leaders and elected officials, as well as personally, between friends and family members.

JOE BIDEN

FORTY-SIXTH PRESIDENT
DEMOCRATIC PARTY
TERM: 2021–2025
YEAR OF THE DECISION: 2024

CIRCUMSTANCE

Born in Scranton, Pennsylvania, Biden moved to middle-class Claymont, Delaware, as a child. He graduated from the University of Delaware and Syracuse Law School. At age twenty-nine, Joe Biden became one of the youngest Americans ever elected to the Senate. Weeks after his Senate election, his first wife and daughter were killed in a car accident, and his two young sons were critically injured. Biden considered abdicating his Senate seat but was convinced otherwise. He was sworn into the US Senate at his son's hospital bedside. He commuted from Wilmington, Delaware, to Washington every day—first by car, and then by train—to be with his family.

Biden was a US senator for thirty-six years, often chairing committees and authoring legislation. He knew the mechanisms of Congress and government well. He ran for president in 2008 but was defeated by Barack Obama in the primaries, who then asked him to serve as his vice president, a position he held for eight years. In 2015, Biden's son Beau died of cancer, leaving the family in a state of mourning during the critical presidential campaign season. For personal reasons, Biden chose to sit out of the 2016 election.

In 2017, Biden was shocked when President Trump did not react to squelch a white supremacist rally in Charlottesville, Virginia. Biden saw this as a moral crisis. Believing a second Trump term would be counter to the country's core values and international standing, Biden announced another run for the presidency in April 2019. He believed the country's political divisions were severe and desired to unify the nation through calm and respectful leadership.

Biden, perceived as left-leaning but overall moderate, eventually won the highly contested Democratic primaries. Many states changed their voting practices during the 2020 election due to the COVID-19 pandemic, especially regarding mail-in voting, early voting, and the delivery of ballots in batches to outdoor vote receptacles placed around cities, making it easier to cast ballots. The election remained too close to call for days, but eventually, Biden was declared the winner.

The new president took swift action to get America vaccinated against COVID-19 and to jump-start the economy through infrastructure projects, environmentally friendly programs, and other initiatives. These created more jobs than any other president had created in a four-year term. Biden's CHIPS and Science Act sought to bring the computer chip industry, which had largely moved to foreign soil, back to the United States. Biden negotiated with large pharmaceutical companies, resulting in lower prescription drug costs for some medications. Biden nominated the first Black woman to serve on the Supreme Court and made a Black and Asian American woman, Kamala Harris, his vice president.

In foreign affairs, President Putin of the Russian Federation invaded Ukraine. Biden rallied America's allies, including NATO countries, to provide military, intelligence, and financial support to Ukraine to slow, stop, and eventually reverse Putin's aggression. As a result, NATO expanded, with formerly neutral Finland and Sweden joining the alliance.

In February 2020, the Trump administration had agreed with the Taliban to withdraw US troops from Afghanistan by the end of August of the following year. Biden's initial goal was to honor Trump's agreement. Biden strongly believed that pulling US forces out of Afghanistan and ending the war there was imperative. The plan was for the US to withdraw gradually while the regular Afghan military ramped up operations to maintain the status quo. This did not happen, though, as the Afghan army almost instantly collapsed, and the ensuing US withdrawal was frenzied. The scene in Afghanistan, especially at airports, was chaotic, although over 120,000 Americans, green-card holders, and Afghans were successfully evacuated. Thousands of Afghans who wanted to leave were left behind. During the withdrawal, a suicide bombing killed thirteen American servicepeople along with numerous Afghans. This tragedy left many in the US questioning Biden's decision-making and so-called expertise in foreign policy.

On October 7, 2023, the Iranian-backed Hamas movement in Gaza attacked civilians in Israel, slaughtering 1,200 Israelis and taking over 200 hostages. Israel responded to this horrific act of terror with an invasion of Gaza in an attempt to root out and destroy Hamas and secure the release of the hostages. The US supported Israel; however, some groups, especially on college campuses, believed Israeli tactics were too extreme, and a pro-Palestinian movement emerged. Other Iranian proxy militias further attacked Israel, and at one point, Iran sent three hundred drones and missiles directly at Israel. Aware that this attack was likely, Biden had already prepared US forces and made alliances with several other Middle Eastern nations to shoot down the missiles as they approached Israel. This was virtually a complete success, with Israel experiencing no substantial damage.

Meanwhile, the terrorist organization Hezbollah's support for Hamas resulted in Israel carrying out a number of covert attacks on and assassinations of Hezbollah leadership in Lebanon, weakening their power in the Middle East. In Syria, a rebel group overthrew the Assad government. Israel took this opportunity to destroy many of Syria's military installations. The Biden administration supported Israel's actions.

On June 27, 2024, CNN held the first presidential debate of the 2024 election. While Trump was more restrained than in prior debates, he espoused falsehood after falsehood. Many in the country were already concerned about Biden's mental acuity, given his age of eighty-one. In this televised debate, the president stumbled over his words and even lost his train of thought on multiple occasions. His energy level, coherence, and ability to think on his feet were questioned, even by his own supporters. These gaffes fed into the belief, especially with conservatives and increasingly with moderates, that the president may not be fit for a second term of the most demanding job in the world.

DECISION

Less than a month after the debate with Trump and amidst tremendous pressure from within the Democratic Party, Biden announced that he would not seek reelection.

IMPACT

About twenty minutes after his announcement that he would not run again, Biden strongly endorsed Vice President Kamala Harris for president.

Within forty-eight hours of Biden's decision, the Democratic Party rallied around Harris, with record-breaking funding and quick commitments from delegates to secure the nomination at the Democratic National Convention.

In a speech to the nation from the Oval Office on July 24, 2024, Biden gave his rationale for his decision, notably mentioning that it was time to "pass the torch" to a younger generation. He outlined his accomplishments and expressed his concern about the potential impact of losing the election to Trump, especially in terms of maintaining democracy. He stated that he decided to put his personal ambitions aside and quit the race for the good of his party and the country.

Biden's decision was a rare instance of a sitting president choosing not to seek reelection. The last one to do so was Lyndon B. Johnson in 1968.

In the 2024 election, Biden's chosen successor, Vice President Kamala Harris, lost to Donald Trump, who, as of this writing, is the forty-seventh president of the United States of America.

DONALD TRUMP

FORTY-SEVENTH PRESIDENT
REPUBLICAN PARTY
TERM: 2025 TO PRESENT

As of the writing of this book, Donald Trump was reelected to the presidency for a second time, defeating Vice President Kamala Harris. Undoubtedly, he will make many consequential decisions during his second term in office. Which will be his most important decision of consequence is yet to be determined.

EPILOGUE

Shortly after the completion of this book, one of the most important decisions of consequence ever taken by an American president was made by President Donald Trump, the forty-seventh Commander-in-Chief. The Islamic Republic of Iran, a nation known for propagating terrorism globally, was in the midst of developing nuclear capability. In June of 2025, over the course of twelve days, the United States and Israel struck Iran militarily with the objective of eliminating its nuclear development program. While this attack was successful, Iran began to rebuild its ballistic missile and nuclear programs.

Following attempts at negotiating to get Iran to cease all atomic development, President Trump, in a stunning decision, ordered the U.S. military to strike Iran in a broad-scale operation, again, alongside the State of Israel. The objectives are to eliminate the political and military leaders of the country, destroy its missile capability, and to permanently and completely obliterate Iran's nuclear program. President Trump has also called on the Iranian people to seize the moment to attempt a regime change to a more Western-friendly government.

As of this writing, this extensive campaign is underway. The United States and Israel have killed over forty of Iran's top echelon of leaders, including the "Supreme Leader." Iran's missile caches are significantly degraded, most of its Navy is sunk, and the rest of its military structure is being reduced to rubble.

In retaliation, Iran is launching drones and ballistic missiles towards American military installations, Israel, and, surprisingly, towards about a dozen of its Gulf state neighbors. Although severely weakened, the remaining Iranian leaders refuse to surrender.

So far, the campaign is an aerial attack with no U.S. troops battling on the ground in Iran. As I write this epilogue, the war is ongoing, and the outcomes are still unknown. One thing is certain: President Donald Trump will be forever known for taking a consequential decision that will change not only the Middle East but the world.

PRESIDENTIAL FUN FACTS

PRESIDENTS BY PARTY AFFILIATION

PARTY	NUMBER
None	1
Federalist	1
Democratic-Republican	4
Democrat*	16
Republican	20
Whig	4
National Unity	1

* Counts Cleveland and Trump Twice

TERMS IN OFFICE

PARTIAL-TERM PRESIDENTS

- William Henry Harrison served the shortest term, lasting only one month in 1841 before dying of pneumonia.
- Andrew Johnson served a partial term after Abraham Lincoln's assassination.
- James A. Garfield served for just over six months in 1881 before being assassinated.
- Zachary Taylor served from March 1849 to July 1850, dying of acute gastroenteritis while in office.
- John F. Kennedy served two years and ten months before being assassinated in November 1963.
- Chester A. Arthur completed three years and five months of Garfield's term after his assassination.
- Millard Fillmore served the remainder of Zachary Taylor's term from July 1850 to March 1853.
- Lyndon B. Johnson served the remainder of Kennedy's term and was then elected for one full term of his own.
- Gerald Ford served a partial term after Richard Nixon's resignation, though this is not explicitly mentioned in the given search results.

ONE-TERM PRESIDENTS	TWO-TERM PRESIDENTS	THREE-OR-MORE-TERM PRESIDENTS
John Adams John Quincy Adams Martin Van Buren Franklin Pierce James Buchanan Benjamin Harrison William Howard Taft Calvin Coolidge Jimmy Carter George H.W. Bush	George Washington Thomas Jefferson James Madison James Monroe Andrew Jackson Ulysses S. Grant Grover Cleveland* Woodrow Wilson Dwight D. Eisenhower Ronald Reagan Bill Clinton George W. Bush Barack Obama Donald Trump*	Franklin Roosevelt, elected to four terms

* Non-Consecutive

PRESIDENTS WHO LOST THEIR ATTEMPT TO BE REELECTED

YEAR	PRESIDENT WHO LOST	WINNER
1800	John Adams	Thomas Jefferson
1828	John Quincy Adams	Andrew Jackson
1840	Martin Van Buren	William Henry Harrison
1888	Grover Cleveland	Benjamin Harrison
1892	Benjamin Harrison	Grover Cleveland
1912	William Howard Taft	Woodrow Wilson
1932	Herbert Hoover	Franklin D. Roosevelt
1976	Gerald Ford*	Jimmy Carter
1980	Jimmy Carter	Ronald Reagan
1992	George H.W. Bush	Bill Clinton
2020	Donald Trump	Joe Biden

* Assumed the presidency when Nixon resigned but was never elected vice president or president.

VICE PRESIDENTS WHO ASSUMED THE PRESIDENCY AND LATER WON ELECTION IN THEIR OWN RIGHT

- Theodore Roosevelt: Became president in 1901 after the assassination of President William McKinley. Elected to a full term in 1904.
- Calvin Coolidge: Assumed the presidency in 1923 upon the death of President Warren G. Harding. Elected to a full term in 1924.
- Harry Truman: Became president in 1945 after the death of President Franklin D. Roosevelt. Elected to a full term in 1948.
- Lyndon B. Johnson: Ascended to the presidency in 1963 following the assassination of President John F. Kennedy. Elected to a full term in 1964.

VICE PRESIDENTS WHO RAN FOR THE PRESIDENCY

VPS WHO RAN AND WON	VPS WHO RAN AND LOST
John Adams (1796) Thomas Jefferson (1800) Martin Van Buren (1836) Grover Cleveland (1892)* Richard Nixon (1968)* George H.W. Bush (1988) Joe Biden (2020)* *Not elected immediately after being VP.	George Clinton (D-R, 1908), not nominated John C. Breckinridge (So. D, 1860) Charles W. Fairbanks (R, 1916) Thomas R. Marshall (D, 1920), not nominated John Nance Garner (D, 1940), not nominated Henry A. Wallace (Progressive, 1948) Alben W. Barkley (D, 1952), not nominated Richard Nixon (R, 1960) Hubert Humphrey (1968) and (1972, not nominated) Walter Mondale (D, 1984) Dan Quayle (R, 2000) Mike Pence (R, 2024), not nominated Kamala Harris (D, 2024)

PRESIDENTS WHO DIED WHILE IN OFFICE

DIED IN OFFICE	CAUSE	YEAR
William Henry Harrison	Pneumonia	1841
Zachary Taylor	Gastroenteritis	1850
Abraham Lincoln	Gunshot	1865
James A. Garfield	Gunshot	1881
William McKinley	Gunshot	1901
Warren G. Harding	Heart Attack	1923
Franklin D. Roosevelt	Cerebral Hemorrhage	1945
John F. Kennedy	Gunshot	1963

UNSUCCESSFUL ATTEMPTED ASSASSINATIONS		
Andrew Jackson	Gunshot	1835
Theodore Roosevelt	Gunshot	1912
Franklin Roosevelt	Gunshot	1933
Harry Truman	Gunshot	1950
Gerald Ford	Gunshot	1975
Ronald Reagan	Gunshot	1981

PRESIDENTS WHO WERE RELATED TO EACH OTHER

DIRECT DESCENT

- John Adams (second president) and John Quincy Adams (sixth president): Father and son.
- George H.W. Bush (forty-first president) and George W. Bush (forty-third president): Father and son.
- William Henry Harrison (ninth president) and Benjamin Harrison (twenty-third president): Grandfather and grandson. Cousins
- James Madison (fourth president) and Zachary Taylor (twelfth president): Second cousins
- Theodore Roosevelt (twenty-sixth president) and Franklin D. Roosevelt (thirty-second president): Fifth cousins
- James Madison and James Polk (eleventh president): Second cousins, once removed
- Martin Van Buren (eighth president) and Theodore Roosevelt: Third cousins, three times removed
- Martin Van Buren and Franklin D. Roosevelt: Third cousins, four times removed
- John Adams and Calvin Coolidge (thirtieth president): Third cousins, five times removed
- James Madison and Barack Obama (forty-fourth president): Third cousins, nine times removed

In total, twenty-one states have been the birthplace of at least one US president.

Virginia:	8 presidents
Ohio:	7 presidents
New York:	5 presidents
Massachusetts:	4 presidents
North Carolina:	2 presidents
Pennsylvania:	2 presidents
Texas:	2 presidents

Each of the following states each produced one president: Arkansas, California, Connecticut, Georgia, Hawaii, Illinois, Iowa, Kentucky, Missouri, Nebraska, New Hampshire, New Jersey, and South Carolina.

PRESIDENTS WHO CHANGED THEIR NAMES

BIRTH NAME	USED NAME
Hiram Ulysses Grant	Ulysses S. Grant
Stephen Grover Cleveland	Grover Cleveland
Thomas Woodrow Wilson	Woodrow Wilson
John Calvin Coolidge	Calvin Coolidge
David Dwight Eisenhower	Dwight Eisenhower
Leslie Lynch King, Jr.	Gerald R. Ford
James Earl Carter Jr.	Jimmy Carter
William Jefferson Blythe III	Bill Clinton

LEFT-HANDED PRESIDENTS

- James A. Garfield
- Herbert Hoover
- Harry S. Truman
- Gerald R. Ford
- Ronald Reagan
- George H.W. Bush
- Bill Clinton
- Barack Obama

PRESIDENTS WHO HAVE WON THE NOBEL PRIZE

PRESIDENT	YEAR	NOBLE PRIZE	REASON
Theodore Roosevelt	1906	Peace	Negotiated an end to the Russo-Japanese War
Woodrow Wilson	1919	Peace	Established the League of Nations
Jimmy Carter	2002 (after presidency)	Peace	Human rights
Barack Obama	2009	Peace	Strengthening diplomacy

ABOUT THE AUTHOR

Forrest Tower is the debut author of the *American History in a Nutshell* series, of which U.S. Presidents is the inaugural topic. *Quotes of Consequence*, and *Successes and Failures* are also part of the series, and all three titles are currently available. Forrest holds a BS from the State University of New York, Stony Brook, and an MS from Wilmington University.

Learn more about the series at
AmericanHistoryinaNutshell.com
or scan the QR code below:

www.ingramcontent.com/pod-product-compliance
Lightning Source LLC
LaVergne TN
LVHW041928090826
845145LV00017B/2296

* 9 7 8 1 9 6 6 1 3 6 1 2 5 *